Live Life on Purpose:

From Discovery to Practice

by

Samuel L. Jones

TELEMACHUS PRESS

LIVE LIFE ON PURPOSE: From Discovery to Practice

The publisher does not have any control over and does not assume any responsibility for author or third-party websites or their content.

Cover designed by Telemachus Press, LLC

Cover art:
Copyright © Thinkstock/470464987/mycola

Published by Telemachus Press, LLC
http://www.telemachuspress.com

Visit the author websites:
http://www.drsamueljones.com
http://www.lifechangingpresentations.com

ISBN: 978-1-941536-30-8 (eBook)
ISBN: 978-1-941536-31-5 (Paperback)

Version 2014.08.05

Printed in the United States of America

10 9 8 7 6 5 4 3 2 1

Live Life on Purpose: From Discovery to Practice will help you release your secret purpose by applying these strategies to discover, define and practice your purpose in life. Don't leave success (in life, business, and relationships) to chance! This book is a great tool to help you discover, define and live life on purpose!

Dedication

THIS BOOK IS dedicated to my grandmother, Melissa 'Madea' Shelton (1925–2004), who epitomized *Living Life on Purpose*. She taught me how to have joy, how to show great resolve and commitment to whatever task was at hand. Her efforts always consisted of discovering, defining, and doing her life's purpose.

My fondest memories of her were when she took me fishing and she was as happy as could be sitting on her bucket waiting for a fish to bite. I did not know it then, but that was one of the most precious gifts a grandparent could give. It was important for me to see her enjoy her time doing something she loved as she taught small, valuable lessons about life. My grandmother's integrity, humility, love and compassion for people left an indelible impression on my life. I will be eternally grateful for her example. I know that I now *Live Life on Purpose* because of the strong foundation.

To my wife, Sarah, the woman of my dreams and my best friend, I dedicate this book and my life to you. I am deeply thankful for my great fortune to be married to you. After fourteen years of marriage, you continue to inspire me be to become a better man. You are my most enduring supporter for anything I put my hands to. Not only did you provide emotional support throughout the writing process, but you helped me arrive at many of the ideas that are reflected in this book. I believe this book would have only been a dream if you were not in my life. My ultimate definition of success is that your spouse loves and respects you even more as the years go by. Needless to say, you make me proud to stand as your king, as I know that you're proud to stand as my queen.

And last, I dedicate this book to my Lord and Savior. You said that if I commit my works to you, you would establish them and make my plans succeed. You are the ultimate Faithful One, and I have witnessed that you do not lie. You always follow through on what you say you will do and as you remind me in your word, the Kingdom of Heaven is at hand. So this book is dedicated to you, the Creator of the heavens and the earth.

Acknowledgments

TO SAY THIS book is by "Samuel L. Jones" overstates the magnitude of what this book is about. Without the significant contributions (the kindness, patience, and hard work of many people and the whispered prayers of many more) made by several people, this book would certainly not exist. There are so many people who played a part in making this book a reality. I have been blessed with so many wonderful people who have made such an impact on my life that trying to name them all is very intimidating (I'm worried that I'll leave someone out).

First, I want to express gratitude to my co-editor Jennifer Arndt. At each stage of the editorial process for each chapter, Jennifer has been insightful, meticulous, and tenacious in her enthusiasm for this project. I believe she understood what I was trying to accomplish with the book before I did, and she gently, but firmly, brought me into line whenever I strayed from my own voice. I want to thank her for the sacrifice she made with her family to complete this project.

Next, I want to thank my high school basketball coach Willie E. Thomas, who saw something in me way before I would believe it. He has been a constant example of what a man should be. I've always appreciated his honesty and the challenges he placed before me. His impact on my life will always be present.

In addition, I want to thank my mother and stepfather, Girte and Samuel Jones. It's always good to know that I can hear you say 'I love you.' For we know that God has blessed our future. I also want to thank my parents-in-law, Dorothy and MC Clark. Even though the law says that I married into your family, your love, support and encouragement has made me feel as if I was born into the family. I appreciate you being God-fearing people, and you will always have an impact on my life because I see you as parents.

Next, I want to thank all of my professional colleagues from the National Speakers Association chapter in New Orleans. Every month, I learn so much from each of you in finding my place in the speaking industry. You continue to believe in me and I know that our voices are making a difference in the world. Special thanks to Bruce S. Wilkinson and Richard Melancon from the NSA chapter in New Orleans. Both of you were instrumental in some aspect of developing the most important components of *Live Life on Purpose*.

Also, I would like to thank, a tireless educator, author and business school professor, Dr. Dennis Kimbro. Your motivation and encouragement in this process made all the difference in the world for me. All of your books pointed me in the right direction to look within myself in order to extract the keys that underlie accomplishment and success. Your words continue to change my life and I say 'Thank you.'

And last but not least, I want to thank my spiritual leader and Pastor Reverend Dr. Walter L. Moore. Your Godly insight, your inspiring sermons and your friendship have constantly fueled my desire to be a God-fearing man. Thank you for your continued support of my mission in life.

Foreword

I'VE ALWAYS FELT that successful leaders are successful readers; leaders learn daily, not in a day, and that the more you read the better you'll lead. But if you're like me, there's only so much time in a day for personal development, so the books you're reading had better grab you, keep you engaged and deliver great value with usable information. Well that's exactly how I felt when I first read *Live Life On Purpose,* by Dr. Samuel Jones, on a long trip to deliver a keynote on the west coast. What was most surprising to me was that I was inspired to read it again, on the way home, with a highlighter and journal in hand.

There are few things more powerful than finding out what your purpose is in life, and Dr. Jones' book helped validate my belief that I was living mine, but I needed additional information. His wisdom, words and actions helped me to further define my purpose, realize its true meaning; and more than that, how to apply it to myself while making a difference to others. I always thought that true learning takes place when education meets experience. This book gave me an education that was an experience!

But what's even more exciting is that I was able to remember the exact moment that I discovered my true purpose while reading when Samuel found his own, awaiting a potential hurricane. It was about ten years ago and I had just walked off stage after delivering an opening conference keynote, and after answering some questions, I could see a young lady waiting to talk to me after everyone had left. She tearfully mentioned something I had said that inspired her to reach out to her sister, whom she hadn't talked to in a few years due to an angry disagreement. As she gave me a hug and walked off, the meeting planner who had been listening nearby said, "You must be very proud that your specific words touched her and inspired her to mend fences with her sister." I said, "I sure was because I didn't say that in my presentation." It was at that point that I knew I was truly living my purpose, because most people can tell the difference. You see, you can't motivate someone to do something that they don't want to do, but an authentic purpose-driven communicator can inspire people to do things they didn't think they could do-or maybe even what they really didn't even want to do. I knew then that my purpose was to have a profession where I could make a living while making a difference at the same time. And as I told the meeting planner, the young lady did not actually hear me say what she thought I said. I explained that she heard what she needed to hear, from the right person, when she was ready to hear it. Now that's a purpose I can live with!

Live Life on Purpose is more than just a book. It's a spreadsheet for the rest of your life and a plan on how to apply it with a three legged stool of passion, practice and proof, with feedback and personal commitment. After studying my journal notes from that plane ride, I now realize where I have both failed and what I have accomplished with the days I have lived and what I want to accomplish with the days I have left, without knowing how many they are. One voice, one message and a sense of the messenger's authenticity can bring purpose to the reader and the listener, when they are ready. It's time to stop getting ready to get ready and read this book with a highlighter and a journal and find yours.

Bruce S. Wilkinson, Certified Speaking Professional
Wilkinson Seminars and Presentations
Professional speaker, trainer and author of *The Thermostat Leader*

Live Life on Purpose:

From Discovery to Practice

Introduction
Purpose is a secret because …

'EXCUSE ME, I have something to tell you. But I don't want you to tell anyone, it's a secret.' Have you ever heard these words? If you haven't, you'll eventually hear them at some point in your life. *Live Life on Purpose* is just the opposite. The purpose of this book is to help you identify the many 'secrets' of your purpose in life and to encourage you to live them out so that the world will be a better place. *Live Life on Purpose* will have you discover the facts and faith you need; it will help you define the meaning of your facts and faith as to how they can motivate you to act; and then it will provide you with some strategies to apply the actions needed to transform your private secrets into public purpose.

According to the Merriam Webster dictionary, a secret is defined as *something kept from knowledge or view or something designed to elude observation or detection.* In my words, a secret is something that you find out that you're supposed to keep to yourself. But I'm hoping that each word; each sentence; each paragraph; each page; each chapter in this book all reveal some secrets to all the readers. The underlying framework for this book is based on three important components to purpose: Self-discovery; define meaning, and the courage to act on what you know or learned. During the course of the book, each of these components will be broken into smaller sections to emphasize their importance.

ough *Live Life on Purpose*, I want you to focus on
hich everyone should embrace, each of which
aced, and respected, these interactions will allow
revelations that will change your life. No matter
, or what we have, we can never avoid them. These
interactio... r people, and the environments we live, work and
play in. A couple of things I've learned is that you can't avoid any of these
interactions, and that they play a major role in the type of person that you will
become. Therefore, the main thing is that we must feed the belief in self,
which eventually affects the other two (other people and our environment).

Accordingly, how do we believe in self? For me, believing in self is a choice
and an attitude that you develop over time. Some call it self-esteem, self-
confidence, or self-assurance. No matter what you call it, it's a freedom
from doubt in your personal abilities, talents and skills to accomplish your
desired goals. The main reason why I'm sharing this is because I didn't always believe in myself or my abilities. It took trial and error for me on several occasions to gain the confidence that I have today. For example, I can
remember taking speech 101 at the University of Southern Mississippi in
the fall of 1993. I would eventually receive a 'D' in that class. Keep in mind,
I was a college athlete (basketball player) that was always put in front of the
TV camera for an interview after the game. Looking back on that today, I
realized that I wasn't a confident public speaker. At the time, I just thought
I didn't like being in front of the camera. A year later, I retook the class and
got an 'A.' What happened? I eventually challenged my own thoughts about
my inability in that area to give myself the confidence to do the thing I
thought I couldn't do. Now, I'm a confident professional speaker, and I'm
thrilled that I challenged myself to overcome my fear and lack of confidence. Ralph Waldo Emerson once said, "The greater part of courage is
having done it before." As for me, fear of doing something can only be
cured by doing it, And soon my confidence was built by doing it again and
again. By doing this, I've been able to have a more positive image of myself
and the public speaking aspect of my life, which is part of the foundation of
my purpose. There's an African proverb that says, "If there's no enemy
within, the enemy outside can do you no harm." That's something I try to

keep in mind whenever I have doubts about my abilities now. T
you try things, the more you learn in the process.

The next interaction that we should all embrace in order to be exposed to
the revelations that will help us change our lives is the interactions and influence of other people. Please know that you can't live alone in this world.
It's good to have support of family, friends, and colleagues at work, but it's
also important to know how they influence you in life. The following two
stories summarize this point:

* The first story ... a small boy once had a cage full of sparrows.
  Hoping to teach the sparrows to sing, he put a canary in the cage
  with them. After a few days later, the boy came running to his
  mother crying, "Mom, the canary is chirping like the sparrows."

* The second story, three male freshmen college students found
  themselves stranded on an island after a night of partying during
  spring break. After searching for something to drink, they found
  a bottle to see what type of drink it was. After a few rubs, a genie
  appeared to grant them three wishes. The first student wished
  that he was home with his girlfriend. Poof, he disappeared! The
  second student wished that he was in Hawaii on a family vacation. Poof, he disappeared! The genie said okay, there's one more
  wish. The third student made a wish. "Okay, I wish that I had
  both of my friends back here with me."

The moral of both of those stories is that whoever you surround yourself
with will eventually influence you in some way. The good book says for us
"not to be misled: bad company corrupts good character." (NIV, 1
Corinthians 15:33) Hence, if you're going to embrace the interactions and
influence of other people, be sure that those that you surround yourself
with will be those that can make you a better person. 'For as iron sharpens
iron, so one person sharpens another.' (NIV, Proverbs, 27:17)

And the last interaction that we should all embrace in order to be exposed
to the revelations that will help us change our lives is the interaction and

ment. Most people don't realize that your envi-
lly the primary source of your belief system. That
so it's based on your desires of what you want to

___, a poor kid in the ghetto can dream of overcoming that life
style, or a rich kid in the suburbs can imagine life as easy and simple because of the resources he had growing up. I've learned that it's all in what
you pursue. The environment you were raised in can either magnify your
dreams and goals or it can smother them. Just know that the environment
you're raised in is NOT the only factor that will help you change your life.
If it was, then every child growing up in poverty would only know poverty,
and every child growing up in wealth would only know wealth. The point is
that we should expose ourselves and our children to both poverty and
wealth, for example, so that they can be exposed to different experiences,
which will help them learn a variety of beliefs. In time, hopefully they can
gain revelations to understand what life is truly about. If we don't expose
them to different experiences or if we're not exposed to different experiences, those secrets will remain hidden, and we won't have a clue as to what
those types of experiences mean to us personally. If you don't expose yourself to new and different experiences, then you'll never have new and different expectations.

So, how could someone's purpose only be a secret? It would be a secret
because we sometimes fail to express the true revelation of who we are,
what we see, what we know, what we've experienced and how we can be of
service to others based on our own revelations. After reading *Live Life on
Purpose*, it is my hope that you express every purpose that is applicable to
you in your life. And once you 'Live it,' it will no longer be a secret.

And in that continuous pursuit of living my purpose, I've been able to discover, define and follow through on the actions needed to transform my
life. Hopefully, the stories and examples in this book will give you some
insights and revelations to your secrets, which will help you *Live Life on
Purpose*. Now that my secret is out, I hope your life will be changed! So keep

turning the pages to see the other secrets that are out there. And once you are aware of them, don't keep it a secret. As a famous song of legendary American singer and film actor Francis Albert "Frank" Sinatra says, "The best is yet to come." And I believe that best is in you, so go *Live Life on Purpose*!

Dr. Samuel Jones
Life Changing Presentations
Professional speaker, trainer, author of *The Man I Never Knew*

Chapter 1
Purpose

Before I formed you in the womb I knew you. Before you were born I sanctified you.
I ordained you a prophet to the nations.

—*Jeremiah 1:5 (NKJV)*

DID YOU KNOW the word "purpose" has power? Whenever I think of purpose, I think: Why am I here on earth? I think about why I am here in this country. I think about why I'm here in Mississippi or in this community. Have you ever thought about the purpose for your life? Have you ever thought about why you were born into the family you're in? Why you live where you live? Why your parents are who they are? Or better yet, why you're not as tall and athletic as someone else? It's very easy in our society to feel compelled to compare ourselves to other people, to want what they have, and to want what they have accomplished. But, we need to remember we are here for a purpose, and that purpose is unique to each of us. Some things we'll eventually get the answers to, and some things we'll have to keep seeking in order to reach an understanding.

If you have ever thought about all those things, as I have, you've probably been busy with trying to make a living instead of making a life, as I once had been. I often had thoughts like these because I didn't always know my purpose in life. I had been previously confused as to where purpose comes from. I had always thought that purpose comes from what I did in life rather than who I am. I had questions like these because I used to only focus on what happened to me. Over the years, I've learned that it's not what happens to me, but it is how I feel about what happens to me. Now I remember to focus on the fact that EVERYTHING happens for a reason and a purpose, and it serves me. But the key to it all is seeking out those reasons and purposes in order for them to serve you. The goal of *Live Life on Purpose* is to help you find the purpose for which you were created. And once you find your purpose, I can promise that your life will be enriched with fulfillment, aspirations, and achievements. Optimistically, everything I share in this book will help you know the reasons and purposes for your life experiences. I also hope these examples serve others in helping them find the path that's most effective for their life. Therefore, in order to make the best of this book, we'll first look at the decision making process and dissect a few cases to make the most of analyzing events that happen and how to make them work for us.

According to the Oxford Advanced Learner's Dictionary, the term "decision making" means *the process of deciding about something important, especially in a group of people or in an organization.* Researchers also define the decision making process as *the selection of a course of action from among two or more possible alternatives in order to arrive at a solution for a given problem.*[i] Therefore, based on both definitions above, a course of action has to be taken in order to reach a decision after some event has occurred. In reality, as long as we live, events will happen in our lives and we'll have to figure out the reasons and learn how they can serve us. Our decisions will be based on information that is in the form of data, facts, or beliefs, and we will have to determine if the information is true or false. All of this information will not be useful unless it is analyzed and processed properly. If we don't understand the true purpose, this information will not be used correctly.

You might be thinking: How do you analyze and properly process information? The best way to do that is to be sure you try to deal with what has happened. I try to encourage people to see things for what they are, but (don't see them as worse than they are) Sometimes when bad things happen, we tend to be irrational about what really happened. For example, you're working late, and you're ready to get home. Just before you leave the office, your spouse calls to ask you to stop at the store to pick up an item. An irrational response will cause you to be agitated and disturbed about such a small chore, but a rational response will be for you to help out. But what if in this same scenario your spouse asks you to pick something up after you've just gotten home from working late instead of calling you before you left the office? Once again, an irrational response will encourage you to make a "mountain out of a mole hill" just to let your spouse know she could have called earlier. See how this one scenario can be taken way out of context if you don't deal with what is *actually happening*? *I can't do Any thing About it*

One of the main reasons why most people see things as worse than they are and have trouble analyzing and processing a situation is because they've developed what psychologists call "learned helplessness." Researchers have determined that learned helplessness is the belief that our own behavior does not influence what happens next; that is, behavior does not control outcomes or results.[ii] Individuals who are affected by learned helplessness usually experience uncontrollable events, from the past and the present, which cause individuals to expect future lack of control.

The learned helplessness response pattern was discovered accidentally during the mid-1960s in a study of animal learning. Psychologist Martin Seligman observed that after exposure to inescapable electric shock, some dogs passively accepted the shock, even when they could take action to turn it off. The so-called helpless dog puzzle initiated decades of research and multiple theories on learned helplessness, which covered various topics including passivity in laboratory rats, clinical depression, children's classroom behavior, success in selling insurance policies, and mortality in nursing homes.[iii]

As an African American, I always try to look back through history to learn from some of the events that may have happened to our ancestors, or just other examples of people with stories of great personal triumph. Of course, this is easy to do during specific holidays or the month of February because it's Black History month, which is celebrated across the country. But I also try to learn from other people's stories because I believe the lessons are applicable and that every race and ethnic group can learn from the past. I truly believe that events in black history, just as events in Hispanic history, Jewish history, and other cultural histories, are definitely things that happened for a reason and a purpose, which can serve mankind. French aristocrat, writer, and poet Antoine de Saint-Exupery said, "It is only with the heart that one can see rightly; what is essential is invisible to the eye."[iv] I believe that we are not here to make this world right, but we are here to see it right. And the best place to start is with our hearts.

One great example of this is the life of one of the most revered and admired winners of the Nobel Peace Prize, Nelson Mandela. Mandela was arrested and imprisoned for twenty-seven years in his home country of South Africa, but he was originally sentenced to life in prison. Mandela used this opportunity to grow as a person; he consistently refused to compromise his political position to obtain his freedom. Prior to and after his release on February 11, 1990, he committed his life's work to uniting his country by standing against the anti-apartheid government. He was elected as the first black president of South Africa in 1994.[v] "Mandela: His 8 Lessons of Leadership," a *Time* magazine article by Richard Sengel, gives a great account of some leadership lessons Mandela learned over time. I believe these lessons on leadership can help us all learn how events can serve us.

- Courage is not the absence of fear—it's inspiring others to move beyond it.

- Lead from the front—but don't leave your base behind.

- Lead from the back—and let others believe they are in front.

- Know your enemy—and learn about his favorite sport.

- Keep your friends close—and your rivals even closer.

- Appearances matter—and remember to smile.

- Nothing is black or white.

- Quitting is leading too.[vi]

Nelson Mandela is a perfect example of how to
you become a better person. Mandela applied
discovering who he wanted to be, by defining th
perience (what it all meant), and by deciding how this situation would help
him become the best person he could be, he understood that his purpose
was greater than the situation he was placed in and greater than the people
who put him there. Mandela passed away in December 2013 just before I
finished writing this book. The world is now left with the wisdom of his
impressionable words by reminding us how to endure hardships and how to
navigate those indescribable situations in life.

Please consider what situation you might be in right at this moment. Have
you considered how this event/situation can make you a better person?
Have you looked at other people who were in similar situations to see how
they were successful through it? These are just some things you might want
to consider as you live through your experience. I want to encourage you to
grow through your experiences, not just go through them. As Marxist theo-
rist, philosopher, economist and revolutionary socialist of Polish Jewish
descent Rosa Luxemburg said, "Those who do not move, do not notice
their chains."[vii] As long as you're making progress, the chains of life have
no choice but to fall off. So keep moving forward, no matter how fast or
slow. Keep moving.

Viktor Frankl is another excellent example of a person who discovered his
purpose through a life event. A renowned psychiatrist, Frankl endured years
as a Nazi concentration camp inmate during the Second World War.
Frankl's experience taught him that a man's primary motivational force is
the search for meaning and purpose, especially when going through pain
and agony. Frankl describes his experience in *Man's Search for Meaning* In
reading his work, I learned three things about his dramatic experience. First,
those who lost faith in the future were doomed to be stuck in their present
situation, and they didn't survive. This theory is supported by French Nobel
Prize winning author, journalist, and philosopher Albert Camus who

man devoid of hope and conscious of being so, has ceased to
to the future."[viii] So once you have a mental decay of hope, it won't
long before your physical attributes will follow. Secondly, for those who
survived the concentration camp experience, it didn't really matter what
they expected from life, but what mattered was what they expected from
themselves. Frankl described how he had looked forward to being free and
sharing his experience with the world. He realized that he expected some
great things of himself because he wanted to share his experience to help
people. And thirdly, this concentration camp experience was one of many
ways that life yells and/or whispers at us to take full responsibility so that
our purpose can be revealed. When I say that life yells and/or whispers at
you, I mean that life demands that we respond with certain actions based
on what is happening to us at any given time. As Frankl insisted:

> Everything can be taken from a man but one thing: the last of the
> human freedoms—to choose one's attitude in any given set of
> circumstances, to choose one's own way ... Even though living
> conditions (lack of sleep, insufficient food and various mental
> stresses) may suggest that the inmates were bound to react in
> certain ways, in the final analysis it becomes clear that the sort of
> person the prisoner became was the result of an inner decision
> and not the result of camp influences alone.

I'm convinced that when we can take the responsibility to find the right
answer to the problems we face, our purpose and task at hand will be ful-
filled as individuals. As I've said, I've learned that we're not here to right all
the wrongs in this world, but we're here to see all the wrongs in this world
in a right way. And how do we do that? Just know that it's not what happens to us, but it's how we respond to what happens to us. And in the end,
that is truly when we find our purpose in life.

Or better yet, let's take on the essence of attitude with the words from Dr.
Charles Swindoll:

> The longer I live, the more I realize the impact of attitude on life.
> Attitude, to me, is more important than facts. It is more

important than the past, the education, the money, than circumstances, than failure, than successes, than what other people think
or say or do. It is more important than appearance, giftedness, or
skill. It will make or break a company ... a church ... a home.
The remarkable thing is we have a choice everyday regarding the
attitude we will embrace for that day. We cannot change our
past ... we cannot change the fact that people will act in a certain
way. We cannot change the inevitable. The only thing we can do
is play on the one string we have, and that is our attitude. I am
convinced that life is ten percent what happens to me and ninety
percent of how I react to it. And so it is with you ... we are in
charge of our attitudes.

Now I know you might be thinking, "I don't want to experience a concentration camp for my purpose to be revealed to me." What if you lose someone you love? What if you lose an arm or a leg? What if you lose your voice
and you make your living as an actor? Or what if you lose your job that
you've had for twenty-four years and you're one year from retirement? How
would you respond to any of these examples? While those examples might
not compare to a concentration camp, they are examples of events we can't
control. The point is that life is going to scream and whisper at us to grow
more causing our purpose to be revealed so that we can achieve things
we've never dreamed of. I believe that life recognizes the gifts that are
within us, which we've been blessed with. But in order for us to achieve the
goal of making our gifts come to life, we must develop the capacity to endure the process. And that is the journey to discovering our purpose.

I learned to endure this process growing up in the Mississippi Delta with
my grandmother Melissa "Madea" Shelton. The first thing to know about
the Mississippi Delta is that it isn't really a delta. The Mississippi River delta,
the mouth of the Mississippi, is actually about three hundred miles south of
where I grew up. The area that I'm referring to as the Mississippi Delta lies
between the Mississippi and Yazoo rivers out to Interstate 55 from
Vicksburg, Mississippi, all the way to Memphis, Tennessee. If you're ever
driving through the area, you'll know you're in a different part of
Mississippi because it's very flat. The area was leveled by the great flood of

1927, which occurred when the levees broke. This is why the area is called the Mississippi Delta, and it's also why the area has very fertile soil for agriculture. When I was small boy, there were fields of crops as far as the eye could see. Every direction I looked, I would see flat, dusty fields. During that time no other area of the country probably better represented the South than the Mississippi Delta.

The Mississippi Delta is a very unique place—people from all over the world travel thousands of miles to sample this remarkable region. I'm always proud to return to see what's changed and what thankfully hasn't about this authentic slice of America.

Living with my grandmother was always interesting. My grandmother raised me while my mother was attending Jackson State University in Jackson, Mississippi. Everybody in the family called my grandmother Madea. She was the original Madea, way before Tyler Perry's character. She was a very stern person who said what she meant and meant what she said. She was always concerned with me doing my best. She constantly said to me, "Sam, if you're going to be a garbage man on the garbage truck, be the best garbage man there ever was." She believed in doing things right and doing things to the best of her ability, and it was important to her that I also learn to do so. This came from a person who did not have a formal education, but she was wise beyond her years.

And as you can probably guess, my grandmother was the one who recognized the gifts inside of me. She always wanted me to do my best no matter what I was doing. My grandmother held me to high standards and those standards have been the tools utilized to develop the capacity to endure the process of life pressing and polishing the greatness out of me.

As I share my thoughts now, I can see the results of her labor in my life as I think about all of my previous work experience. I've been able to learn from all the jobs I've ever had, and that's a revelation within itself. I can vividly remember my first official job where I got a weekly pay check. That job was "chopping cotton." Chopping cotton isn't really chopping down cotton plants. The work involved in chopping cotton is to hack away at the weeds that are growing on the rows where the cotton is planted. If the weeds are not chopped out, they will overtake the cotton plant and stunt its growth. Visualize this with me: It's about 100 degrees (even though it seems like 105–110 degrees with the humidity); you're dressed in blue jeans, a long sleeve cotton shirt; you have your garden hoe in hand; you work from 6 a.m. to 5 p.m. with a forty-five minute lunch break. The field you're chopping in is about twenty-five acres. (Thinking about that now, I'd hate to think how many rows of cotton that is.) And the last few details: You're 12 years old, and this is your summer job. Once again, according to the standards of my grandmother, you're going to work hard and you're going to act like you like it.

I worked hard and I acted like I liked it, but only on the outside. On the inside I was thinking, "I don't want to do this for the rest of my life." Later on in life, before my grandmother passed away, she and I were sitting on the top floor of Reed Green Coliseum after one of my basketball games at the University of Southern Mississippi. My grandmother came to several of my games there and she would always be in her wheelchair on the top floor. Sometimes I wonder if she could even see the game, but it just felt good knowing that she was there to support me. That really meant a lot. After one of my games, we were sitting on the top floor and talking, and it just hit me to ask my grandmother why in the world she made me chop cotton at the ripe old age of 12. She replied, "I wanted you to appreciate hard work and to get your education. I knew you had a lot of great potential in you, but I wanted you to turn your potential into standards and hard work. You don't develop your potential until your reach down into the core of your soul and what you think you can't do. You don't know what you're capable of doing until you try."

What great words of wisdom. That one conversation with my grandmother stayed with me even as I continued in college and worked at several other jobs in my career. I learned life lessons in all the jobs I've had. (See Figure 1.)

Job	Lessons learned
Chopped cotton	I did not want to do this for the rest of my life.
Mowing grass	The importance of quality, neat work.
Sporting goods store	Different sports/personalities of people, i.e. soccer moms.
Sold vacuum cleaners	To accept rejection.
Plywood factory	I did not want to do this the rest of my life.
UPS	The importance of taking care of other people's property.
Sunbeam assembly line	How my work made someone else's job harder or easier.
Structure (now Express Men)	To be neat in appearance, compliment people, be sincere and make sales.
Professional basketball player	The importance of listening to that inner voice and always believing in myself.
Assistant basketball coach	The importance of the details of practice.
Assistant Dean	How to help people succeed.
Dean	How to lead myself before I could lead others.
Business owner	How to identify potential opportunities.

Figure 1. Jobs that have taught lifelong lessons.

I've had a lot of different jobs, and I've been able to learn not only something about the particular job, but I've been able to learn about myself, as well. I believe the ultimate goal in life is to learn something about ourselves through our life experiences. We do not give ourselves enough credit about making it through tough situations to become better people. I can appreciate the person that I am today, but I can also recognize that I still have

much to offer because there is so much more in me that I can
prehend yet. The reason why I can say that is because my soul i ....p. telling
me that my purpose is still growing. And as long as it's growing, it's still
alive.

Is your purpose still alive? If you're not sure, let me give you some advice to
help you get some clarity as to how you can either discover, define, or decide what your purpose is in life. Would you agree that the world of tech-
nology has given us the blessing and curse of constant communication?
We're always connected to family, friends and the world by way of technol-
ogy via cell phones, the internet, television, and other means of communication. And if we're not careful, we could spend our lives distracted and end
up watching other people's dreams come true because they found their
purpose in life. The best advice I can give you in order to know your purpose, to know if it's growing, or to know if it's still alive is to simplify your
life.

When I say simplify your life, I mean to find yourself in your thoughts, your
mind, your soul, your spirit. The way we currently communicate with each
other, it's hard to find a free moment without someone text messaging,
emailing, or calling on our cell phones. But the freedom revelation for me is
that I can choose when to reply or respond to all those things that pull at
me. The choice is up to me, as it is up to you.

French mathematician, physicist, inventor, writer, and Christian philosopher Blaise Pascal was correct when he stated, "All of man's troubles stem
from his inability to sit alone, quietly, in a room for any length of time."
The best way to truly understand the world is to remove yourself from it;
and in doing so you begin to understand yourself. And when you understand yourself, that's when you discover, define, and decide what your purpose is in this world. Canadian psychotherapist and writer Nathaniel
Branden, author of *Honoring the Self: Self-Esteem and Personal Transformation*,
insisted, "The task of consciousness is to perceive that which exists, to the
best of our ability. To honor reality—the perception of that which exists—
is to honor consciousness; to honor consciousness is to honor the self."[ix] I
call this basic time to think about who you are and what you want your

future to be. Henry Ford once said, "If you don't think about your future, you won't have one."

Vince Lombardi, legendary Hall of Fame football coach of the Green Bay Packers, was once asked why he chose to have his championship team run so many simple sets of plays when there were so many versatile and outstanding players with so much talent on the team. He responded, "It's hard to be aggressive when you're confused." So how can you discover your purpose, how can you define the meaning of your purpose, and how can you decide how to move forward with your purpose if you're confused? The answer is you can't! The first place to start is to simplify your life. And this is what I've been able to do by thinking long and hard about my journey to grow as a man. During the past ten years, I have discovered my purpose through my passion for serving and helping people and the knowledge of knowing I'm in the right area for my gifts. This is my life's purpose, simply put, and it is the core foundation for everything that I do:

> I change lives with words. I use my voice and the written word as
> an instrument for change. I encourage, motivate, and inspire my-
> self first, and my purpose is to do the same for others. That's my
> purpose!

If you take the time to seriously consider the gifts and talents that you have, you'll definitely be on the fast track to finding your purpose. I didn't always know what my purpose was. As I said earlier, the main reason why I didn't know what my purpose was early in life was because I really didn't know where purpose comes from. I assumed that it came from outside of a person, or that the type of work that we do or did created our purpose. My lack of understanding at that time reminds me of the story about a man crawling on his knees looking for his lost keys under a street light on a cold winter night. A stranger eventually showed up and offered to help him find the lost keys. After both men had been frantically searching to find the keys for about an hour, the stranger asked, "Are you sure you lost your keys out here?" The other man replied, "No, I know I lost my keys in my house, but the reason I'm looking here is because there is more light out here under the street light." I can honestly say that this example fit me when I didn't know my purpose. I was just like this man who lost his keys in his house but focused on where the light was. I had focused on all the things that were in the light during that phase of my life when I got a lot of attention.

My light compared to the street light was the fact that I was considered by some to be a great athlete. I played high school basketball and ran track; I played college basketball at a major Division I institution; and I was able to play professional basketball in Finland. This was the light because I was always getting attention for being an athlete. Athletes are always getting attention from friends, family members and particularly out in the community, especially in a place like the Mississippi Delta. I can remember hearing people in the grocery store say things like, "That's the guy who signed a basketball scholarship with USM, and he is good. He might even go to the NBA." At the time, comments like this were blowing my ego up because I was in the limelight. The funny thing now, as I look back, is that I've always known that I wanted to be seen as more than just an athlete, but it was hard for me to recognize that at the time. That was my purpose whispering to me, letting me know that greater things were in me than just being an athlete. The athletic journey played a major part in me finding my purpose, so it's not all bad.

What is your street light today? What are you clinging to in order to avoid going to the place where you know you lost your keys (your purpose)? Are you doing things right now that bring you the limelight? Are you doing things just so you can hear people brag about how good you are? Or can you admit that you don't know what your purpose is? Can you be honest with yourself? I encourage you to really consider these questions.

Robert Roots, author of *Success Secrets from The Three Little Pigs*, maintained that it's not what you don't have that keeps you from being successful or happy in life, but it's what you think you need. Search for the truth in your life and face it head on. Facing the truth is the first true reality of finding your purpose. Understand and know that you'll have to face your fears before facing the truth; have courage to pursue these thoughts. Writer Ambrose Redmoon said, "Courage is not the absence of fear—courage is the judgment that what you want is more important that your fear."[x] It has taken me consistently having the courage to stand on my purpose, and that has made all the difference in the world for me.

Accordingly, as you continue to read this book, have the courage to go inside your home, your heart, your soul, and your mind to truly find your keys (your purpose). It is my hope that this book will help you to do the following: First, to motivate you to discover your purpose; second, to encourage you to define your purpose; third, and most importantly, to inspire you to live your purpose. If you truly take to heart the message in this book, you will have accepted the invitation to live life on purpose. I say, "Welcome to the journey!"

Chapter 2
Discover Your Purpose

All truths are easy to understand once they are discovered;
the point is to discover them.

—*Galileo Galilei*

I CAN STILL remember the exact day I discovered my purpose. It was a warm, humid Sunday morning in South Mississippi on August 26, 2012. When I first woke up on that morning, my mind was focused on a few things. The first thing on my mind was the fact that I was grateful to see another day that the Lord had made. And, among other things, I was focused on attending worship service for the day. We have Sunday school or church service every Sunday, so I was looking forward to the message that would be delivered for the day. And the final thing that was on my mind was Hurricane Isaac. Hurricane Isaac was a storm looming in the Gulf of Mexico along the same path as one of the most destructive hurricanes in American history, Hurricane Katrina.

Ever since Hurricane Katrina in 2005, whenever there is the slightest thought of a tropical storm or a hurricane headed to the Gulf of Mexico, the Gulf region is always on pins and needles preparing for the worst case scenario. And we have every reason to be on pins and needles because

Hurricane Katrina killed more than eighteen hundred people and caused at least one billion dollars in damage.

Hurricane Isaac was looming on a similar path as Hurricane Katrina during about the same time of the month. And before Hurricane Isaac would reach the coast of Florida on this particular weekend, it would have already claimed six lives in Haiti. Weather experts were expecting Isaac to become a Category 2 hurricane with "extremely dangerous" sustained winds of 105 miles per hour before it would reach the Florida coastline. Needless to say, on this particular morning I had a lot on my mind, but I knew that there would be something different about this day.

Also on this day, my pastor, Dr. Walter L. Moore, was at his friend church in Columbia, Mississippi, preaching for an anniversary service. Columbia is known as the birthplace of NFL Hall of Famer Walter Payton. It's definitely a great place to visit and to enjoy the hospitality of South Mississippi. At the time of this anniversary service I was still serving as a deacon, so I was used to supporting my pastor while he was speaking at other churches. Normally I liked to help start the service when we visited other churches, but for some reason, on that day I could not get there early to save my life.

As my wife and I entered the sanctuary, the service had already started and we made it there just before my pastor stood to start his sermon. And just before he started, I got this excited feeling as if something special was going to happen on this day. It's really hard to explain. My pastor was introduced, and then the congregation sang "Amazing Grace." Then my pastor prayed, gave his text, and then gave his subject. The subject for his sermon on that day was, "Empty, but need to be filled." As I write this now, I know I'll never forget it. After that point in his message, I don't recall any words that he said. The reason I don't recall any specific words is because God spoke to me through this sermon, and that was the day that I found the purpose for my life. The entire time my pastor was preaching this message, God the Father, the Son, and the Holy Spirit preached this same message to me, but it was changed to, "Filled, and need to be empty." As I sat there with tears streaming down my face, I experienced a feeling as if I was a newborn baby wrapped in the hands of God. I sat on the pew with tears still flowing;

God's soft spoken voice came to comfort me during this spiritual roller coaster. I needed to be comforted because I was pondering so many thoughts in my heart and mind. I deliberated, "Is this true? Why me? Why now? Can I do this? I'm not a good speaker." I felt like Moses at the burning bush when God told him to go and speak to Pharaoh. Like Moses, I was contemplating: "Who am I? Who should I say sent me?" And just like with Moses, God would put all my concerns and excuses, all my fears, and all my doubts to rest when he said to me, "Go, and preach my word to those who are lost." That faithful day my life took an elevated path because it was the day that I accepted my call by God into the ministry to preach the Word of God.

Have you ever encountered an experience that changed your entire outlook on life? If you haven't, I hope my experience can help you envision greater things for your life. As I share this now, it makes me realize that I never envisioned myself becoming a minister. I had never even envisioned myself becoming a deacon at a church prior to doing so. In other words, I really haven't envisioned myself doing a lot of the things I've done in my life. The reason I share this with you now is because it's important to know that everything you've encountered or been through, it's been for a reason and a purpose. I've discovered that those life changing moments occur only to serve to help you discover your purpose.

I want to be blunt and upfront. In order for us to truly discover our purpose, we need to take charge of our lives by taking charge of our thoughts and by having the courage and fortitude to take our lives to another level. I'm reminded of what Paul said in 1 Corinthians 2:9, "But as it is written, eye hath not seen, nor ear heard, neither have entered into the heart of man, the things which God hath prepared for them that love him" (KJV). This is one scripture that encouraged me to pursue my purpose once it was made known to me. In order for me to discover my purpose, I had to do the following four things before this process could evolve: **I had to overcome fear; I had to constantly expose myself to positive messages; I had to raise my standards; and I had to learn to focus more on what's important in life.** I hope that as I address these components, they will help you discover your purpose.

Overcome Fear

There is no illusion greater than fear.

—*Lao Tzu*

Polish physicist and chemist Marie Curie said that nothing in life is to be feared, it is only to be understood. Curie became the first woman to win a Nobel Prize and the only woman to win the award in two different fields (physics and chemistry). Even though her work was considered to be dangerous and unexplored, it led to the discovery of polonium and radium and the development of x-rays. Knowing how dangerous Curie's work was under those conditions, some would be afraid to work with those kinds of materials today. Can you envision something you fear daily that you might not think about? The older I get, the more it seems that each sunrise brings new reasons to fear something. These are some of the things I've heard people say they are afraid of:

- They're afraid of constantly rising gas prices.

- They're afraid of the latest stories on the evening news because ninety-nine percent of the stories are negative and contain bad news.

- They're concerned about unemployment because it seems to be at an all-time high.

- They're afraid they will have just enough left over from one pay check to make it to the next and an unforeseen emergency could arise.

- They're afraid their children will not have the same opportunities they've had.

- They're afraid of the rumors of possible layoffs at work, and no one knows whose name is on the list.

- They're afraid the government is going to take away their freedoms.

- As litigation rates have risen across the country, they're afraid of being sued.

- They're afraid of finishing last in class.

- They're afraid of finding out if that mole on their arm is cancerous.

And sometimes, we all fear the sound of the clock as it ticks, signaling we are getting closer to the grave. The point is that we all have had things in life that we've feared, and in reality it's going to take faith to overcome all of those fears.

As for me personally, the main issue I had on my journey to discovering my purpose was the fear of public speaking, which is known as glossophobia. Studies show that people fear public speaking more than death. And based on that research, it seems to me that most people would rather be the one in the casket than the person speaking the eulogy. That pretty much summed up my fear of public speaking until I truly discovered my purpose. According to the National Institute of Mental Health, almost three fourths of Americans suffer from speech anxiety, more than five million people have some type of social phobia, and at least three million people have a fear of crowded or public places. As you can see, there are a lot of people living with fears.[xi] (See Figure 2.)

Fear of Public Speaking Statistics	Data
Percent of people who suffer from speech anxiety	74%
Percent of women who suffer from speech anxiety	75%
Percent of men who suffer from speech anxiety	73%

Figure 2. Fear of public speaking is very common.

I never really had to deal with public speaking until my sophomore year at the University of Southern Mississippi. I sat motionless in the public speaking class as the instructor discussed the assignments on the syllabus. I was shocked with nervousness, stress, and anxiety as I constantly worried about standing in front of strangers and speaking about any given topic. I was really making this a bigger ordeal than what it was. The class met every Tuesday and Thursday morning at 9:30 a.m. The anxiety I was feeling was so bad, I felt as if I was going to have a heart attack as I walked to class each day. I constantly played these thoughts over and over in my mind: "What if I have to speak in class today? What if I can't remember what to talk about? What if I can't get the words out? What if they laugh at me if I start to stutter? What if ... what if ... what if ...?" The "what if's" were really feeding the fears that I already had. I really don't know how I managed to get through the course. I struggled through the class and eventually ended up with a final grade of D.

There were two main reasons why I struggled in this class. I had a severe stuttering problem, and I lacked the self-confidence needed to stand before perfect strangers and speak my thoughts. It really didn't dawn on me until I was being interviewed after one of our basketball games that I really needed to overcome my fear of public speaking, which led to the growth of my confidence. I owe most of my current confidence and desire to take chances with public speaking to Mitch Williams, who worked for local television station WDAM as a sports journalist. He had the charisma to make any seemingly embarrassing moment feel as if it never happened. Williams could always get his interviewees to open up and smile as he called their names before he started the interview. As he began asking me questions about the game we had just played, he would always ask something that would make me loosen up. It was just something about the way he looked at me that gave me confidence to speak to the camera as if the camera was my best friend. Williams would always end my interviews with me by saying, "We're going to make you look good and sound good, Sam, so don't worry."

Looking back on that now, it was just Williams's belief in me that allowed me to believe in his belief in me. Sometimes we have to believe in someone else's belief in us before we can believe in ourselves. And to this day, I don't think that Williams knows the impact he's had on my life. The semester after that first interview with Williams, I retook the public speaking class and got an A. That one experience led me to define F.E.A.R. as False

Expectations Appearing Real. In this class I had been focusing on all the "what if's" of public speaking instead of on the things that I could do. That's what those false expectations will do. One of my favorite African proverbs states, "If there's no enemy inside, the enemy outside can do you no harm." I was actually my own worst enemy the first time going through this class. And the most important thing, whether it's a fear of public speaking, fear of heights, fear of flying, or anything else that you can think of, and we all have something we're afraid of, it is of the utmost importance to recognize a fear so that you can overcome it. The success of tomorrow will always depend on the work of today so continue to keep fighting off fear with faith.

Psychologists have found that we're all born with two types of fears: the fear of falling and the fear of a loud, sudden sound. Any other fears outside the scope of those two, we learn and we cause them to become part of our mental, emotional, and physiological makeup. I find it amazing that the Bible speaks of two types of fears also, a commanding fear and a forbidden fear. An example of a commanding fear would be Proverbs 1:7, "The fear of the Lord is the beginning of knowledge ..." and Ecclesiastes 12:13, "Now all has been heard; here is the conclusion of the matter: Fear God and keep his commandments, for this is the duty of all mankind." (NIV) I believe the commanding fear is a fear of reverence and respect for who God is. I believe we should all have this fear because we should show honor and respect to God at all times.

An example of the forbidden fear would be Psalm 91:5, "You will not fear the terror of night ...," and 1 John 4:18, "There is no fear in love. But perfect love drives out fear, because fear has to do with punishment. The one who fears is not made perfect in love." (NIV) Therefore, fear is something that is very real, but we must be aware that we have the ability to control it. I like what Will Smith's character, Cypher Raige, said in the 2013 summer blockbuster movie *After Earth*. He contended, "Danger is real, but fear is a choice."[xii] And Greek Philosopher Epictetus said, "Men are not afraid of things, but of how they view them." Whatever we're afraid of today, we must decide to view differently, and we'll be amazed as to how our fears will slowly creep away.

We have to make the conscious decision to work through our fears each day. One strategy I've learned is to talk to myself to be sure that my thinking is in line with my faith and not in line with fear. This is something that I've had to learn to do for myself. It's always good to get encouragement from others, but we also need to be able to encourage ourselves. William Shakespeare wrote in *Julius Caesar*, "A coward dies a thousand times before his death, but the valiant taste of death but once ..."[xiii] He was really saying that every time we fear something, it's like we're dying many deaths because we're not having faith. George Patton said, "Fear kills more people than death."[xiv] Psychologist Nathaniel Branden said, "Fear and pain should be treated as signals not to close our eyes but to open them wider."[xv] I'm glad that I've allowed fear to help me not only open my physical eyes, but to open my spiritual eyes by learning to have more faith than fear.

Whenever I'm in a situation where fear tries to be the voice of the hour, I talk to myself and say, "It's not what you think it is. It's not that bad. There's some good in this, you just have to look for it." For example, I've had to constantly talk myself through several memorable situations. First, I dunked in the wrong goal during an exhibition game while playing for the University of Southern Mississippi. Yes, it was stressful, and I was embarrassed as my teammates gave me a hard time in the locker room, in the dorm, and even out on campus. But even as I was the punch line in all the jokes, I always knew that I could find some good from the experience, and I constantly reminded myself of the lesson I learned. Now I share this story with my audiences so they, too, can learn from it. And you might be thinking, what can I learn from someone dunking in the wrong goal? It all started when the center on the basketball team lined up on the wrong side of the court, which led me to line up on the wrong side of the court. The morale of the story is to be careful about who you follow, for they might lead you to dunk in the wrong goal.

Another situation I had to talk myself through was when I first started the doctorate of philosophy program at Mississippi State University. I had a lot of doubts and fears at the beginning of the program, but I continually talked to myself to insist that I could do the work and that I belonged in the program. The first semester of any doctoral program could be very intimidating, but the confidence that I gained as I presented my my dissertation motivated me to finish the program in three years though I had a full-time job.

Probably one of the proudest moments I had experienced having confidence in myself was in accepting the call into the ministry. Yes, that fearful voice did try to talk me out of embarking on this honorable path, but it was faith that sealed this deal for me. I've learned the best form of faith is to know. My faith in knowing my purpose, and knowing that the voice of God put that fearful voice to rest because I was assured by the Holy Spirit that this was my calling and purpose. The only true way to cure the fear of doing something is to do it. And each time you do it, your confidence will grow, and your fear will be destroyed little by little.

Another strategy I've used to overcome my fears is to use my imagination. Merriam-Webster defines imagination as 'the act or power of forming a mental image of something not present to the senses or never before wholly perceived in reality.' I like that definition, but I like mine better. I define imagination as 'using my thoughts, my words, and my body language to create and to bring forth spiritual things into the natural realm for any given experience.' We really can't do anything we can't picture ourselves doing. That's the way we are with fear. As humans, we try to control our fears. That's why scary movies are so popular. In June of 2013, there were at least twelve scary movies scheduled to be released before the end of the year. When I was younger, I watched them because I knew I had control over frightening scenes; I knew that it was only a movie. I enjoyed the adrenaline rush of being afraid in a controlled environment. But once the movie was over, I knew I wanted to go back to my regular and normal life of freedom and control.

Currently, I use my imagination for something good rather than for something limited to entertainment. If you're trying to be faithful in your thoughts, actions and behaviors but you're watching things that are fearful, try to use your imagination to think about things that will benefit you. Ralph Waldo Emerson said, "A man is what he thinks about all day long."[xvi] As I said at the beginning of this chapter, we have to overcome fear in

ose. Allow your fear to grow your faith into what
er to reveal your purpose. We'll always be placed
to see how much faith we truly have. Once we
th we have, we discover that fear doesn't have to
. Hence, when we choose to overcome our fears,
we'll be one ... ep closer to discovering our purpose, as French
philosopher Guillaume Apollinaire said:

"Come to the edge," he said. They said, "We can't. We are afraid."

"Come to the edge," he said. They said, "We can't. We will fall!"

"Come to the edge," he said. They came. He pushed them. And they flew.[xvii]

Michelangelo said, "Most people fail in life not because they aim too high
and miss, most people fail in life because they aim too low and hit; and
some never aim at all." And what keeps people from aiming? Fear! Fear
eventually leads to low aim or no aim. One of my favorite quotes from Dr.
Benjamin Mays summarizes the thoughts on fear and low aim. Mays was
seen as a giant in Christian ministry as well as American education, and he is
remembered for his work as a preacher, mentor, teacher, scholar, author,
and activist in the civil rights movement. When it comes to fear and low
aim, Mays insisted:

"It must be borne in mind that the tragedy of life doesn't lie in
not reaching your goal. The tragedy lies in having no goal to
reach. It isn't a calamity to die with dreams unfulfilled, but it is a
calamity not to dream. It is not a disaster to be unable to capture
your ideal, but it is a disaster to have no ideals to capture. It is not
a disgrace not to reach the stars, but it is a disgrace to have no
stars to reach for. Not failure, but low aim is sin."[xviii]

Exposure to Positive Messages

The only thing worse than being blind is having sight but no vision.
—Helen Keller

"Sunlight is the best disinfectant," is a well-known statement m[...]mer U.S. Supreme Court Justice Louis Brandeis.[xix] Brandeis was[...]and associate justice on the Supreme Court of the United States fro[...]to 1939. He used this line to refer to the benefits of openness and transp[...]ency in the operation of the government. Well, as individuals we can appl[...]this simple principle of being open and transparent with our thoughts as we attempt to discover our purpose. In the case of discovering my purpose, the best sunlight that I've been able to use to disinfect my mind was constant exposure to positive messages. I've learned that without the constant exposure to positive messages, I will eventually believe the negative messages that surround me. For example, without constantly reading positive things (such as stories in the Bible, or autobiographies, and other books and articles on leadership and personal development), I would have eventually focused on things that don't encourage perseverance or faith. Focusing on things such as the downfall of the economy or the rising crime rate or on the rumors of wars and famines in other countries don't encourage perseverance or faith. I'm not saying that we should be like an ostrich and stick our heads in the sand, but I am saying that in order for us to discover our purpose, we must find positive messages to be exposed to so that our purpose will come into view. As it states in Proverbs 23:7, "For as a man thinketh in his heart, so he is." (KJV) We'll be whatever we think about, which is why it's good to have our minds exposed to positive thoughts. American industrialist Henry Ford said, "Whether you think you can, or you think you can't—you're right."[xx] Nepalese poet, writer, and researcher Santosh Kalwar insisted, "We are addicted to our thoughts. We cannot change anything if we cannot change our thinking."[xxi] And former Egyptian President Anwar el-Sadat said, "He who cannot change the very fabric of his thought will never be able to change reality, and will never, therefore, make any progress."[xxii]

I found two principle ways to expose myself to positive messages, which have helped me to discover my purpose. I discovered these principles when I was completing my master's degree in public relations at the University of Southern Mississippi. The first principle was to control the messages that I chose to believe based on my own thoughts, remarks from others, or the

25

ated from the environment that I'm in. In the
l, this is considered 'top of mind awareness.'
en a brand or a specific product or service
nen thinking of a certain industry. The term
verdi, former president of the National Retail
...ncil and owner of a prestigious marketing and advertising
gency in New York.[xxiii] Companies now spend billions of dollars to build
top of mind awareness through media exposure on the radio, the television,
the internet, and more commonly now on social media sites. One of the
most expensive rates for top of mind awareness advertising is for airtime
during the Super Bowl. According to an article in *The Huffington Post*, the
average cost for a 30-second Super Bowl ad spot in 2013 was roughly four
million dollars, which was $500,000 more than the previous year.[xxiv] And in
an article in *Forbes* magazine, experts in the industry predict that it's only a
matter of time until the advertising market for Super Bowl Sunday hits ten
million dollars for a 30-second Super Bowl ad.[xxv]

The Super Bowl ads are perfect examples of how much advertisers are
willing to pay to get that top of mind awareness. And since marketers are
trying to control their messages to their customers, it's up to us to control
the messages that we want to receive. These marketers are not spending this
money to show they like their customers. They are spending this money to
affect behavior, to get customers to have top of mind awareness so that
when it comes time to purchase products, customers will remember and
respond with their pocketbook.

As individuals seeking to discover our purpose in life, we have to take control of the messages that we choose to believe. Everyone will respond accordingly with behavior that matches the message that is received. If we
constantly hear messages that tell us that we need the latest fashion or the
latest gadget, then we'll be more likely to act on those messages. And if
we're living pay check to pay check, and we know we can't afford the latest
fashion or gadgets, based on those messages we could spend the last of our
money trying to keep up with all the latest trends. When we ensure the flow
of only positive messages through our minds, the behavior we respond with
will be positive; and in turn, this positive energy will keep us on a path to

discovering our purpose. An example of a positive message could include knowing we can't afford to spend our money on all the latest gadgets right now, but that what we do have is enough.

The second principle way in which I expose myself to positive messages in order to discover my purpose is to consistently seek out positive messages. We're more than likely consistent with the things we do well and inconsistent in the things we don't do well. Author, motivational speaker and business owner Anthony Robbins insists that it's not what we do once in a while that shapes our lives, it's what we do consistently. In the book *Outliers*, author Malcolm Gladwell popularized the "10,000-hours rule," which dictates that it takes about ten thousand hours of practice to become an expert or to achieve mastery in any given field. Gladwell came up with the rule by studying the lives of extremely successful people to find out how they had achieved success.[xxvi] Even though some have taken the 10,000-hours rule out of context, the point of the rule is to convey that no matter what area you want to be great in, you must consistently practice. In this case, you must practice using positive messages and keeping your mind and thoughts on a positive plane.

As for finding my purpose in my life, I've had to consistently expose myself to positive messages because there were so many negatives messages that were sent by my subconscious mind. One negative message that I was consistently faced with came in the form of a question: "How are you going to inspire, motivate and encourage other people if you don't even know who your biological father is?" As I shared in my first book, *The Man I Never Knew: How Leadership Can be Developed by Faith, Family and Friends*, the hardest part about not knowing who my biological father is has been the struggle to understand how I've become the man I am today without having him in my life. These thoughts didn't really become as important until I reached adulthood and began to have the desire to start my own family. Not having my father in my life while I was growing up had a huge impact on me. I never had a birthday party with my father. I never went fishing with my father. I never saw him smile when I scored my first points on the basketball court. I never got that encouragement of a hug or heard him say the words, "Son, I'm proud of you." And even through the process of writing my second book, I still wonder if he even knows that I exist. Since those are things I've always wondered but I never got answers to, it's important for me to consistently expose myself to positive messages. And probably one of the most positive lessons I've learned from not knowing my father is that this has forced me to look within myself to discover who I should become. So I no longer look at this experience as a curse. I see this as something that has encouraged me to continue to use my response as an example of faith, courage, and strength.

A favorite story, which helps me to continue to expose myself to positive messages and deal with negative experiences that I have no control over, is the Bible story of Joseph. This story exemplifies how we can face adversity and still come out victorious. We need to always recognize that everyone will face adversity at some point in his or her life. I've learned that who you are on the inside as you go through trials and tribulations will always determine how you face those trials and tribulations. In the Bible, Joseph, the son of Jacob, was despised by his brothers because of the dreams that he received from God. Joseph knew that God had given him dreams and visions of how he would become a great leader, but he was prideful and arrogant about it. This led his brothers to leave him in a pit to die, which led to him being sold into slavery. He then worked for Potiphar who trusted him with all of his property, but he was soon wrongfully cast into prison by Potiphar for the attempted rape of Potiphar's wife. Joseph had plenty of reasons to be angry, to be resentful, or to seek revenge. Instead, Joseph always chose the high road. Whenever I'm in situations where I have no control, I tell myself to take the high road because I'll never have to worry about a traffic jam. When we do the right thing, we won't have to worry about everybody running to our rescue. We just have to know that we can get through it because we know we're focused on the right message. I have found as I continue to study the inspiring story of Joseph that there are **six positive character traits: acknowledgement and acceptance, persistence and determination, patience and endurance, integrity and honor, humility, and forgiveness and compassion.**

Acknowledgement and Acceptance

Most often one of our first responses to adversity is to ask ourselves, "why me?" I'm learning more and more each day that accepting the circumstances that I'm in helps me to better face the trial. By accepting his status as a slave, Joseph simply goes to work for Potiphar, where he eventually proved himself to be a good worker with a great attitude. Potiphar recognized Joseph's value and rewarded his righteousness by entrusting his entire household to Joseph as chief steward. After Potiphar's wife falsely accused Joseph of rape, Potiphar cast Joseph into prison for several years. In all of his trials, Joseph immediately got over these road blocks to accept the situations as they were. Through all of these difficulties, he continued to remain faithful to his beliefs. Joseph's example showed that the only way to move forward is to constantly accept and acknowledge the trial and tribulation while continuing to focus on what we believe is true. Author J. K. Rowling insisted that understanding is the first step toward acceptance, and only with acceptance can there be recovery.[xxvii]

Persistence and Determination

In every situation that Joseph found himself in, he never sought to undermine or react negatively to those who mistreated him or enslaved him. Whether it was his brothers, Potiphar, or Potiphar's wife, or even Pharaoh, he continued to help them to prosper. By focusing on his own commitment to his beliefs, others were able to recognize Joseph's gifts and talents because he was persistent in doing the right thing for God. Former Prime Minister of the UK, (Winston Churchill, maintained that success is stumbling from failure to failure with no loss of enthusiasm.) American poet (Robert Frost vowed that the best way out of something is always through) it.[xxviii] If we don't persist through our trials and tribulations, others may never see our true talents and abilities and the gifts God has given us.

Patience and Endurance

Joseph always knew God was going to bless him because of his dreams, but he didn't quite know when it would happen so he had to endure these trials with patience. But even through this process of patience, he had to seek solutions through the adversity (Isn't it amazing that when we have patience through whatever we go through, we seem to find all the answers we need? And when we don't have patience, we can't seem to find the answers?) It always appeared as if Joseph was forgotten by some people, but he was never forgotten by God. He was forgotten by his brothers when they put him in the pit. He was forgotten by the butler when they were in prison after he interpreted his dream; but most importantly, he was never forgotten by God. Since God will never forget about his children, Joseph showed us how to let the promises of God help us to patiently endure our trials and tribulations. Brazilian lyricist and novelist, Paulo Coelho, maintains that the two hardest tests on the spiritual road are the patience to wait for the right moment and the courage not to be disappointed with what we encounter.[xxix]

Integrity and Honor

Has someone ever tried to get you to do something that is wrong over and over, and over again? If so, did you survive the test? Joseph was placed in this situation day after day when Potiphar's wife attempted to seduce him. Instead of giving in to her request, he fled. This was a test of integrity because no one was around to witness his decision, and he made the correct choice according to his beliefs. British statesman and colonial administrator Lord Milner said, "If we believe a thing to be bad, and if we have a right to prevent it, it is our duty to try to prevent it and damn the consequences."[xxx] Because Joseph didn't accept her advances, his consequence was going to prison, but he was true to himself and to his God. American essayist, lecturer, and poet Ralph Waldo Emerson says, "Nothing is at last sacred but the integrity of your own mind."[xxxi]

Humility

Former President Abraham Lincoln said, "I am not bound to win, but I am bound to be true. I am not bound to succeed, but I am bound to live up to what light I have."[xxxii] In other words, Lincoln was saying that he wanted to live up to the gift that had been given to him through humility. Joseph also showed humility when Pharaoh sent for him to interpret his dreams. Of course, after all that Joseph went through, he could have easily taken credit for his abilities. But instead, Joseph chose to be humble and gave all credit to the Lord. The conversation between Pharaoh and Joseph went like this: Pharaoh said to Joseph, "I had a dream, and no one can interpret it. But I have heard it said of you that when you hear a dream you can interpret it." "I cannot do it," Joseph replied to Pharaoh, "but God will give Pharaoh the answer he desires."[xxxiii]

It's apparent that Joseph had learned through all of his adversities that it was God who was blessing him through his trials and tribulations and not due to his own merit. When coming upon a trial, going through a trial, and coming out of a trial, it's important to know that humility helps you to understand we get through only by the hand of God.

Forgiveness and Compassion

Mahatma Gandhi declared, "The weak can never forgive. Forgiveness is the attribute of the strong."[xxxiv] After all that Joseph went through with his brothers, he revealed his identity to them when he was prepared to forgive them for their crimes against him. He told them, "And now, do not be distressed and do not be angry with yourselves for selling me here, because it was to save lives that God sent me ahead of you. For two years now there has been famine in the land, and for the next five years there will be no plowing and reaping. But God sent me ahead of you to preserve for you a remnant on earth and to save your lives by a great deliverance. So then, it was not you who sent me here, but God."[xxxv] Joseph knew that all of his personal adversity had been part of a much bigger picture, and that's how he was able to forgive his brothers freely. American media proprietor, talk

roducer, and philanthropist Oprah Winfrey said, "True
n you can say, 'Thank you for that experience.'"xxxvi
was thankful for his adversity when he gave credit to
Go pose of saving lives. Forgiving others who have seemingly
wronged us he best way to make progress through adversity (Bitterness,
anger, and resentment will keep us from making progress. For adversity
always helps us to develop and grow.)

If we can develop these six character traits, we can face whatever trials and
tribulations come our way with the same grace and strength that Joseph
had, and that will help lead us to our purpose.

Raise Your Standards of Thought

Excellence is to do a common thing an uncommon way.
—*Booker T. Washington*

Whenever I think about raising my standards of thought, I think about
Plato, John Locke, Epicurus, Confucius, and Martin Luther King, Jr., just to
name a few. But one great thinker that I cannot fail to mention is Greek
philosopher Aristotle. Aristotle was a student of Plato and teacher of
Alexander the Great. His writings cover countless subjects, including physics, poetry, linguistics, politics, and government, among others.xxxvii He is
one of the most important founding figures in Western philosophy. One of
my favorite quotes from Aristotle insists that, "Excellence is never an
accident, it's always the result of high intentions, sincere effort, and
intelligent execution; it is the wisest choice of many alternatives; therefore
(choice, not chance, determines your destiny.)xxxviii He maintained that
choosing high intentions, sincere effort, and intelligent execution is what
helps us to raise our standards of excellence with thought. When we raise
our standards of thinking, we will definitely discover our purpose in life
because we raise our standards of thought. The higher we are thinking, the
clearer our vision of our purpose in life will become. I want to share with
you two of my favorite stories about raising our standards of thought and
how their examples give us proof.

The first story is a rag to riches story about author J. K. Rowling of England. The single mother became an international legend in 1999, when her *Harry Potter* series took over the top slots on the New York Times Best Seller List.[xxxix] Rowling began writing at the age of six, with a story called "Rabbit," which she never finished. Throughout her life, her favorite subject was English, and she eventually had a short stint as a secretary for a publishing company. It was during a train ride that she had an idea for a story about a boy who discovered he was a wizard. But this story wouldn't become a book until seven years later. Rowling would eventually get married, have a child, and be divorced shortly after. Faced with poverty and depression, this is where Rowling had to raise her standards in order to complete the manuscript. She would write feverishly in cafés for two to three hours at a time, while her infant child slept next to her. Once completed, the finished manuscript is said to have been rejected up to twelve times. She finally sold the book, *Harry Potter and the Philosopher's Stone* (the word "Philosopher" was changed to "Sorcerer" for its publication in America), for about four thousand dollars in 1998.[xl]

The book was an instant success, earning the UK's National Book Award and a gold medal in the Nestle Smarties Book Prize.[xli] By the summer of 2000, the first three *Harry Potter* books, *Harry Potter and the Sorcerer's Stone*, *Harry Potter and the Chamber of Secrets*, and *Harry Potter and the Prisoner of Azkaban*, earned approximately 480 million dollars in three years, with more than thirty-five million copies in print in thirty-five languages.[xlii] By the time the fourth book appeared in 2000—*Harry Potter and The Goblet of Fire*—the series had become an international phenomenon.[xliii] By 2000, Rowling had become the highest earning woman in Britain, all because she decided to raise her standards to follow her dream of writing children's stories.

Oprah Winfrey interviewed Rowling in 2010. In this interview, each woman spoke candidly, not only about her success, but also many of the emotional challenges she faced. Rowling spoke about all of her insecurities throughout her life. She faced clinical depression after the death of her mother and later after her short-lived marriage. She maintained that divorce taught her that she had an inept survival instinct, which led her to surviving as a single mother on welfare as she pursued her efforts to become a writer. Rowling created the Dementor, a character in the Harry Potter stories, to represent all the dark, lonely days during her depression. But it was the other characters she created in her writings that encouraged her to raise her thoughts of perseverance and hope. She insisted that the only thing she believed in at the time was that if she could get her first novel published, it would be a hit. Rowling stated, "I can remember walking away from the café one day after I was writing. A voice spoke to me that said the difficult thing is to get this book published. If this book can get published, it will be huge." And the rest is history. This one project was the only thing she believed in at the time. She said, "One of the greatest accomplishments of all my writings is to teach readers how to use their imaginations."[xliv] Thank you, J. K. Rowlings! You're forcing your readers to use their imagination because you're an example of what can be done when you raise your thoughts.

The second story is about a man named Bruce Lee, who is known as the greatest icon of martial arts cinema and a key figure of modern popular media. Lee was born in America to a Chinese father and a Chinese-German mother. Shortly after his birth, the family moved back to Hong Kong, where they lived until Lee was nineteen. At the age of thirteen, Lee was beaten up by members of a local Hong Kong street gang, which prompted him to train in Kung Fu. That would be the last fight he ever lost. Lee faced tremendous challenges throughout his life, but it was due to his mindset and focus on his passion that made him become one of the most recognized names throughout the world today, almost forty years after his death.

Lee eventually started a career in acting, which led to a variety of roles in several television series, including *Batman* and *The Green Hornet* and ultimately a few movies. Lee had a couple of things that helped him raise his standards of thought. First he had a back injury in 1970 that nearly cost him his acting career. While lifting weights, he heard a loud popping sound from his back that was accompanied by tremendous pain. This loud popping sound would be the result of damage to a sacral nerve in his lower back. Doctors told him that he would never kick again, and he would be confined to a bed for six months. Secondly, after he recovered a year later, Warner

Brothers decided to go with a Caucasian actor instead. Frustrated at the lack of opportunities in Hollywood for an Asian-American actor, along with the frustration from overcoming an injury, Lee sat down and wrote a letter to himself.[xlv] Reading the letter now shows that he raised his level of thinking by giving himself a goal to aim for. Read his letter and see how you can raise your own thoughts.

My Definite Chief Aim

I, Bruce Lee, will be the first highest paid Oriental super star in the United States. In return I will give the most exciting performances and render the best of quality in the capacity of an actor. Starting 1970 I will achieve world fame and from then onward till the end of 1980 I will have in my possession $10,000,000. I will live the way I please and achieve inner harmony and happiness.

Bruce Lee
Jan. 1969

Lee's last movie was *Enter the Dragon*, and he passed away in 1973. After his untimely death, *Enter the Dragon* was released in the United States and China, and it elevated him to the level of an international star. *Enter the Dragon* was budgeted for $850,000, and as of 2013, it has grossed 25 million dollars in the United States and 90 million dollars worldwide.[xlvi] The story of Lee's letter to himself reminds me to raise my level of thoughts by stretching my goals, my dreams, and my aspirations. I'm reminded that a great ship is not looking for creeks, streams, and ponds to sail in, but only the deepest waters. With that being said, the deeper the water, the deeper my anchor needs to go to handle all the storms. My anchor is my faith, trust, and dependence on God. So let us raise our standards of thought by thinking like Isaiah as he encouraged us: "For my thoughts are not your thoughts, neither are your ways my ways, declares the Lord. As the heavens are higher than the earth, so are my ways higher than your ways and my thoughts than your thoughts."[xlvii]

Focus, Focus, Focus ...

Vision requires hindsight, insight, and foresight.
                                        —*William H. Taylor*

When I hold experiential leadership training sessions, I show a video of adults playing a game and ask my audience to count the number of passes made by a team of three players. There are always two teams of three players participating in the game in the video; one team is in white shirts and the other is in black shirts. The players are passing a basketball back and forth. The task of my audience is to count the number of times the team in the white shirts passes the ball. It's normally a pretty simple task for my audience. It's so simple, in fact, that while my audience almost always gets the number of passes correct, at least seventy-five percent of the audience misses the person in the gorilla suit strolling through the background in the video. It would seem that's hard to miss, but the audience almost always does. In the book *The Invisible Gorilla: How Our Intuitions Deceive Us*, authors Christopher Chambris and Daniel Simons contend that this video demonstrates two important lessons: We are blind to a lot of what happens around us; and we are blind to our own blindness.[xlviii]

Researchers refer to this occurrence as "inattentional blindness." The term was coined in 1998 when psychologists Arien Mack, PhD, of the New School for Social Research, and the late Irvin Rock, PhD, of the University of California, Berkeley, published the book, *Inattentional Blindness*, describing a series of experiments to explain this phenomenon.[xlix]

The explanation is that our mind is constantly overloaded from processing all the stimuli that it takes in. As a result, our mind has built in short cuts to speed up processing time. Because of these short cuts, however, we often only see what we expect to see. So when I show this video in my leadership sessions, my audiences expect to see six people passing a ball, but they never expect to see a gorilla, so they usually don't see it. The following are four criteria that researchers found, which are required to classify or define an inattentional blindness episode:

1. The observer must fail to notice a visual object or event.

2. The object or event must be fully visible.

3. The observer must be able to readily identify the object or event if they consciously perceive it.

4. The event must be unexpected and the failure to see the object or event must be due to the engagement of attention on other aspects of the visual scene.[1]

In my leadership sessions and in real-life scenarios, even highly intelligent people can become so focused that they fail to notice anything outside their expectations. Therefore, this blindness can be damaging to anyone who is trying to discover their purpose in life. Maybe they're so focused on their job that they can't see their true gifts. Or maybe someone is so focused on the negative attributes of someone else that they can't see the love that person has for others. The point of this is to recognize how we can become so blind. Hence, how do we recognize these inattentional blind spots in order to see what we need to see? I've learned that I must focus more on the really important things at hand.

Have you ever been in a conversation with someone who spouts off with their opinion on any subject that's brought up? He or she has an opinion about the weather. They have an opinion about community leaders. They have an opinion on the study of medicine. And they have an opinion on how well the president is doing. More to the point, he normally has an opinion on how bad the president is doing. You get my drift. But as you ponder on those thoughts now, how does it make you feel when someone is just spouting off their opinions on those topics? Does it make you feel good and enthused? Does it make you want to ensure that somebody pay for your troubles? Or does it give you an uncomfortable feeling by zapping all of your energy to where you just feel drained on the inside of your soul?

If we're really focusing on what they're saying, we're probably not going to feel good or enthused unless we agree with them. I've learned that I must focus more on those things that are important to me. And yes, the weather might be really important to someone who's sharing their opinion, but he can't do anything about it. And yes, it might even be important for someone to share their opinion about the president, but what can he do about it? Some say vote the person out of office, but chances are they'll be complaining about the next person elected. The point I'm trying to make is that if we really want to discover our purpose, we're going to have to focus, focus, and focus on the important things, which give us the foundation for our purpose. Motivational speaker and author, Anthony Robbins, maintains (that where focus goes, energy always flows) If we focus on our purpose, we'll have enough energy to pursue our purpose. And if we focus on the negative things in life, we aren't going to have enough energy to keep the negative things from growing.

In this segment, I'll be describing how our focus is more than just for seeing. It is my hope that this section will help you have a focus for how we should pay attention to the people we spend time with and how we actually spend our time. (Time is the only thing that we spend that we cannot get a refund on.) However, don't assume that I'm going to insist that you judge anyone or judge the situations in your life because in the Bible, Matthew 7:1 says, "Do not judge and criticize and condemn others, so that you may not be judged and criticized and condemned yourselves." (AMP) The whole point is to make you aware of how the actions of others can influence you positively or negatively, depending on what you decide to focus on. Greek historian and author Thucydides said, "The bravest are surely those who have the clearest vision of what is before them, glory and danger alike, and yet, notwithstanding, go out to meet it."[li] Therefore, if we have the right focus, then it doesn't matter what we face, who we face, or the depth of the situation, we will come out with the purpose.

One of the many definitions for focus in Webster's dictionary is "the center of activity, attraction, or attention." I believe this is an interesting definition because it implies that we can view a subject or an object from a mental view rather than a physical view. When we focus on something, we either can look at something we don't agree with as a minor situation and make it a major crisis; or we can view it as a major situation, but as no big deal. Either way, exaggerating things or minimizing them can lead to problems, so we need to try to see things for what they truly are. To keep us from aggerating or minimizing things, we must have a clear focus on what's really important.

Whenever I'm learning about my own focus, I try to follow four simple principles: time, subject, message, and response. Keep in mind, to shine the light on self-first, means to be sure we have the right intent in our heart. I'm always focusing on the actions of self-first instead of focusing on the actions of other people. And when I do that, it helps me to keep my purpose at the center of attention in my mind. I haven't always been able to do that, but maturity and life experiences have helped me practice this over and over. My ability to **focus on time, subject, message, and response** has allowed me to consistently recognize a problem while focusing on the things needed to solve it.

Time

The first principle about learning how to focus is to keep time at the forefront. I've been told that time is the wisest of all counselors. When I don't agree with something or I don't like something, I try to determine if this information is important enough for me to learn immediately. I've been surprised at how much time is spent trying to debate something when it's really not that important at the moment. I've learned that some things can just wait and that some things just don't matter. I had to learn this lesson when I first became actively involved in social networking sites like Facebook, LinkedIn, and Twitter. Of course, these sites are tools for interacting with friends and family, but I got lost in the shuffle when I realized how much time I was wasting posting comments on subjects that didn't matter. Instead of working on my speeches for upcoming events or working on my book, I was wasting time on something that didn't support my purpose. Entrepreneur and philosopher William Penn said, "Time is what we want the most but what we use the worst."[ii] I'm learning to use my time wisely and not spend it on things that are not important.

work—it is the price of success.

think—it is the source of power.

play—it is the secret of youth.

Take time to read—it is the foundation of knowledge.

Take time to worship—it is the highway of reverence.

Take time to lend a helping hand—it is the source of joy.

Take time to love—it is the one sacrament of life.

Take time to dream—it hitches the soul to the stars.

Take time to laugh—it is the music of the soul.

Take time to pray—it helps bring Christ near.

—Author Unknown

Subject

The next principle I try to follow when learning about staying focused is getting an understanding of the subject matter that I might be involved with. This is important because this is an opportunity to forge new channels of communication, which will keep us aware of what's happening around us. I try to always gather information from many sources that might cover the topic of my involvement so that I can have some background knowledge. Author Dan Willingham, in the book *Why Don't Students Like School*, stated that background knowledge is necessary for cognitive skills in order to make you a good thinker.[liii] It's important that we become good thinkers when we hear things we might not agree with or those things that just rub us the wrong way. Even though we might not agree with the issues being discussed, it's still equally important to keep our ears open. The more we're in tune and in touch with what is being said, the better we can evaluate the accuracy once we've researched it, and this can give us an accurate account of what we've learned in the process. We can't learn anything when we refuse to hear the other side of an issue. I've learned to tell how big someone's belief in something is by observing how much it takes to discourage them. So, the next time we're offended or we just don't like the way something is being handled, we must focus on the subject and get all the background knowledge we can. In the end, we'll be wiser than we were before the incident, and maybe it will help us focus on our purpose.

Message

The next principle I try to follow is to be focused on the messages that I'm sending when I might not agree with what is being discussed. I've learned to always send a consistent set of messages when I either agree or don't agree with something. It takes a lot of time and energy to have a phony personality. I've always believed that simple, open, and honest messages will minimize stress, confusion, and suspicion. It's easier to just be ourselves. No matter what messages we send, we communicate them in two different ways, internally and externally. Internal messages are communicated by our thoughts, what we read and how we process what we hear. If we don't process them correctly, we will interpret things as what we want to hear. The second way we communicate the messages we send is via external communication: the words we speak out loud, our body language when we agree or disagree with something, our facial expressions, and so on. Our body language can be a dead giveaway, so be mindful because we might have people reading us like a book.

Response

Now that those rules have been applied, the last principle is to focus on our response, which is a follow up from our messages. The quality of the previous three components will be determined by our ability to remain focused with a purposeful response to the challenges, which may come our way. Two of my favorite responses came from two individuals who had some harsh treatment to live through, but yet they both remained focused on something greater. Both gave us an example of how to stay focused so that we could choose our response to any given situation to get our desired outcome.

The first example is the Austrian neurologist, psychiatrist and Holocaust survivor, Victor E. Frankl, mentioned in the first chapter. Frankl poignantly described his experience in a concentration camp during the Holocaust in his profoundly inspiring book *Man's Search for Meaning*. To survive the Holocaust, Frankl would keep hope (and himself) alive by focusing on thoughts of his wife and the vision of seeing her again, and by dreaming at one point of lecturing after the war about the psychological lessons to be learned from his Auschwitz experience. In all of his experiences during his time in the concentration camp, he kept focusing on the fact that he would one day survive the experience in order to help others. In the book he stated, "Between stimulus and response there is a space. In that space is our power to choose our response. In our response lies our growth and our freedom." But in order for him to have this type of response, he had to remain focused on something greater than himself.

The second example is that of Jesus Christ on the cross. I believe Jesus died on the cross to redeem mankind back to God and to save the world from sin through his love. Even in the process of his death on the cross, he was mocked, scorned and tortured as recorded in the Gospels of Matthew, Mark, Luke, and John in the Bible. As described, he was nailed to the cross and hung between two common criminals and suffered an indescribable death. Just before Jesus died on the cross, his first words indicated what type of response he had in his heart for those who were partaking in his crucifixion. According to the Gospel of Luke 23:34 Jesus said, "Father, for-give them, for they do not know what they are doing." (NIV) Could we respond like that if we were in that situation? I don't think I could, but I do know that this is a perfect example of how we should respond when we come up against difficult people or situations. Jesus remained focused even through torture, ridicule, and mockery.

These are two great examples of how we can choose our responses no matter the situation. Both men were able to remain focused even though their situations meant loneliness, pain, and were even surrounded by death.

One thing I've learned from both situations is that nothing has any meaning except the meaning I give it. No matter what is happening to me at any given time, it's completely up to me to remain focused by getting some understanding of the subject matter; it's up to me to focus on the messages that I want to communicate; and it's up to me to focus on what my responses will be.

Once I can focus this process on a consistent basis, I know my light will be powered to shine by itself, but I will have to aim it in all the dark places where the light is needed. As the famous song says, "This little light of mine, I'm gonna let it shine ..." So the secret from this chapter is that you need to know that you have a light, which I call purpose. You just need to be connected to the power source (which is God) and to go and let your light shine by discovering your purpose. Matthew said in the same way, "Let your light shine before men that they may see your good deeds and praise your father in heaven."[liv] (NIV) So as you discover your purpose, you discover life. Go and live life on purpose!

Chapter 3
Discover (The Intelligent Purpose)

If you know heaven made you, then surely earth can find some use for you. So don't worry that you might be poor, and your shoes might have holes in them, and you don't have your dream job, remember to let your mind be a palace of purpose.

—*Dr. Samuel Jones*

IN THE PREVIOUS chapter, I talked about four specific ways for you to discover your purpose. Those consisted of overcoming your fears, constantly exposing yourself to positive messages, raising your standards of thought, and learning how to focus on the things that will bring you the results that you desire. It is my desire that those four ways will assist you in creating the foundation you need in order to build your purpose. Like in construction, the most important section of anything that we build is the foundation upon which everything else will rest. As Jesus taught in the book of Matthew 7:24–27 (NIV):

"Therefore everyone who hears these words of mine and puts them into practice is like a wise man who built his house on the rock. The rain came down, the streams rose, and the winds blew and beat against that house; yet it did not fall, because it had its foundation on the rock. But everyone who hears these words of mine and does not put them into practice is like a foolish man who built his house on sand. The rain came down, the streams rose, and the winds blew and beat against that house, and it fell with a great crash."

Jesus was saying that if your life's foundation is not built on something solid and stable, when the storms of life begin, you will not be able to withstand the test. This assessment also applies to discovering your purpose. If you don't have a solid foundation to build your purpose upon when the storms of life begin, your purpose will not stand. The foundation for your purpose should always be built upon overcoming your fears, constantly exposing yourself to positive messages, raising your standards of thought and continuing to focus on the things that will bring you the results you desire.

Once you have established everything on a solid foundation, then it will be time to move to the next phase of building, which is to discover the process of living your purpose. This is when you analyze your abilities and talents by identifying your learning styles, which I call the "intelligent purpose." I call it the intelligent purpose because I believe that everyone has the capability to be logical, have clear well-processed thoughts, be understanding, communicate with others, and learn. I believe that your purpose should always reflect back to these elements because this is the foundation for your learning style and how we relate to other people.

Researchers refer to these learning styles and elements as intelligence. Developmental psychologist Dr. Howard Gardner argued that intelligence is categorized into three primary or overarching categories, which are formulated by abilities. According to Gardner, intelligence is

1. the ability to create an effective product or offer a service that is valued in a culture;

2. a set of skills that make it possible for a person to solve problems in life; and

3. the potential for finding or creating solutions for problems, which involves gathering new knowledge.[iv]

Gardner summarized this model in his 1983 book *Frames of Mind: The Theory of Multiple Intelligences*. He articulated seven behaviors that were described as intelligence. Since the original conception of this theory, Gardner has added an eighth and ninth behavior.[lvi]

Gardner suggested that there are multiple kinds of intelligence, and everyone has some form of intelligence. The key is to know what your intelligence area is and to focus on that area and to apply the principles to your behaviors. The intelligence theory has had great criticism because psychologists and even educators argue that Gardner's definition of intelligence is too general, and that the nine intelligences simply represent talents, personality traits, and general skills. But even with the criticism, I can see how this can give individuals hope in terms of finding a specific personal area to focus on so they might have success achieving a goal as they live their purpose. Keep in mind, we are all stronger in a specific area, but the key is to know where your intelligence strengths lie. I believe that when you know the areas of intelligence where you excel and you focus on those traits, then you'll be confident to practice using those intelligence styles.

Gardner defined intelligence as a biological and psychological potential to solve problems and to create products that are valued in one or more cultural contexts.[lvii] I believe that arriving at a working definition of "an intelligence" was probably one of the most important steps Gardner took. In his book, *7 Kinds of Smart*, Thomas Armstrong, PhD, also offers a magnificent characterization of intelligence by being a proponent of Gardner's groundbreaking work. Armstrong defines intelligence as "the ability to respond successfully to new situations and the capacity to learn from one's past experiences." Armstrong described Gardner's nine intelligence components as nine "smart" talents. I agree with Gardner's and Armstrong's observations about each of these multiple intelligences, and I call them talents. The nine areas that Gardner describes as intelligence are spatial/visual, linguistic/word, logical/mathematical, bodily/kinesthetic, musical/rhythmic, and interpersonal/working with people, intrapersonal/self, naturalistic/nature, existential /spirituality.[lviii]

Nine Talents

Spatial/Visual Talent: Good with Art and Design

Spatial/visual intelligence is the ability to think in three dimensions. The core capacities include mental imagery, spatial reasoning, image manipulation, graphic and artistic skills, and an active imagination. If you have a strong spatial/visual intelligence, you prefer to use images, pictures, colors, and maps to organize information and communicate with others. A good sense of direction is a key trait of spatial intelligence. If you are talented in this area, it easy for you to find your way around using maps. People with this kind of intelligence may be fascinated with mazes or jigsaw puzzles, or spend free time drawing or just daydreaming. When you're using your visual or spatial intelligence, you'll commonly use phrases such as:

- Let's look at it differently

- See how this works for you

- I can't quite picture it

- I'd like to get a different perspective

- I never forget a face

So if you consider yourself to be a visual learner, use images, pictures, colors, and other visual media to help you tackle a specific task. It's important to incorporate a lot of imagery into your visualizations as much as you can because the more imagery that you have, the more likely you will be to retain the information. And the more information that you retain in the process, the more confidence that you will gain when doing the specific task at hand. Research shows you learn best by:

- using color, layout, and spatial organization in your memories, and using many "visual words" in your assertions such as see, picture, perspective, visual, and map;

- using system diagrams to help you visualize the links between parts of a system, for example major engine parts or the principle of sailing in equilibrium;

- replacing words with pictures, and using color to highlight major and minor links;

- using the visual journey or story technique to help you memorize content that isn't easy to "see."[lix]

Here's a list of artists who used their spatial skills to find their way. Each of them also happened to live with some form of a disability. Their unique combination of intelligences—strengths as well as weaknesses—made them such successful people.[lx]

- **Leonardo da Vinci** was an Italian painter, sculptor, architect, musician, engineer, and scientist. He epitomized the Renaissance Man. Did you know he had a learning disability called dyslexia?

- **Vincent Van Gogh** was a post-impressionist painter, originally from the Netherlands. Van Gogh had epilepsy and struggled with mental illness, including depression and dementia.

- **Marc Chagall** was a Russian cubist and expressionist painter. He had a communicative disorder called Attention Deficient Hyperactivity Disorder (ADHD), which leads to a problem of not being able to focus, being overactive, not being able control behavior, or a combination of these.

- **Henri de Toulouse-Lautrec** was a French painter and lithographer. Lautrec fell and broke both legs when he was a child and his growth was permanently stunted.

Career matches include:

- architect

- graphic designer

- engineer

- fashion designer

- interior decorator

- photographer

People with a strong visual intelligence usually:[lxi]

- seek ocular stimulation;

- respond to color, line, and shape;

- can "see" ideas;

- use mental images for mnemonic devices;

- Imagine possibilities;

- enjoy expressing themselves through the arts;

- appreciate symmetry and congruence;

- enjoy rearranging their environment;

- can manipulate three-dimensional models in their minds;

- understand by seeing a concept in action.

Linguistic/Word Talent: Good with Words

Gardner defines the linguistic/word intelligence as the ability to communicate and understand both the written and spoken word to express complex meanings. Linguistic intelligence allows us to understand the order and meaning of words and to apply meta-linguistic skills to reflect on our use of language. We put them to work whenever we speak, read, write, or listen. Linguistic intelligence is the most widely shared human competence. I believe this is probably one of the most important intelligence areas that will be affected by the emergence of technological devices such as smart

iPad, and other mobile devices because, as a society, this technol-
ogy is encouraging us to use shorthand (shortcuts) in communicating with
each other. For example, here are just a few of the most common abbreviated text messages:[lxii]

- **2moro**—Tomorrow

- **2nite**—Tonight

- **BRB**—Be Right Back

- **BTW**—By The Way or Bring The Wheelchair

- **BFF**—Best Friends Forever or Best Friend's Funeral

- **RBTL**—Read Between The Lines

- **LOL**—Laughing Out Loud or Lots Of Love or Living On Lipitor

- **ROTFLMAO**—Rolling On The Floor Laughing My Ass Off

- **WYWH**—Wish You Were Here

- **XOXO**—Hugs and Kisses

So the next time you get an abbreviated text message, be sure that you understand what the sender is trying to say to you. Based on the examples
above, it's easy to see how the importance of communicating with each
other can be drastically affected. And not only that, this text message lingo
is making its way into the educational system. According to a 2013 news
story in Dougherty County, Georgia, educators are seeing more slang and
grammatical errors in students' writing, and they believe that cell phones
and social networking are to blame. As Andrew Sadler, the seventh grade
reading and language arts instructor at Radium Springs Middle School in
Albany Georgia maintains, "The improper language and improper grammar
with all the texting and using text code is being used to write formal essays.
We recognize that as a school district, we must test, teach, retest, and re-
teach, so that at all times, the students know where they are and what component they need to work on."[lxiii] And surely this is not the first or the last

case of something like this to happen, but it is important to be aware of and face this issue head on. If we don't face this issue head on as a society, we will then be in danger of losing our linguistic intelligence.

People with linguistic intelligence like to play on the meaning or sounds of words and phrases, often using tongue twisters and rhymes. They also enjoy reading, writing, telling stories or doing crossword puzzles. When you're using your linguistic intelligence, you'll commonly use phrases such as:

- Tell me word for word

- The word you're looking for is ...

- I hear you, but I'm not sure I agree

- Let me spell it out for you

- In other words ...

If you consider yourself to be a linguistic learner, use the techniques that involve speaking and writing. You'll have a lot more confidence in your efforts if you incorporate the practice of pronunciations of words, talking yourself through a particular process, or using audio recordings of your conversations for repetition. Researchers insist that linguistic learners learn best by using:

- discussions, dialog, debates;

- oral reading, cooperative learning groups, hearing anecdotes or stories;

- phonics, memorization, listening to tapes or CDs.[lxiv]

Here's a list of people who used words to make a name for themselves. These writers and orators also lived with some type of disability. Their unique combination of other intelligences made them such successful people.[lxv]

- **Agatha Christie** was a legendary British mystery writer. She had a learning disability called dysgraphia, which prevented her from writing legibly. As a result, all material had to be dictated to a typist/transcriptionist.

- **Demosthenes** was a great Greek orator. He had a speech impediment.

- **Edgar Allan Poe** was an American macabre poet and short-story writer. He was emotionally disturbed.

- **Alexander Pope** was an 18th Century British poet and satirist. He had a spinal curvature and never grew taller than four feet, six inches.

- **Rudyard Kipling** was a poet and author of *The Jungle Book*. He was the first English author to win the Nobel Prize in Literature. He was also sight-impaired.

- **John Irving** is the contemporary American author of the *The Cider House Rules* and *The World According to Garp*. He is dyslexic.

Career matches include:

- writer
- editor
- public speaker
- politician
- preacher
- teacher
- journalist
- broadcaster
- English/writing tutor
- actor/actress

People with a strong linguistic intelligence usually:[lxvi]

- appreciate the subtleties of grammar and meaning;

- spell easily;

- enjoy word games;

- understand jokes, puns, and riddles;

- use descriptive language;

- are good storytellers;

- internalize new information through lecture and discussion;

- demonstrate understanding easily through discussion and essay.

Logical/Mathematical Talent: Good with Numbers and Math

Gardner defines the Logical/mathematical intelligence as the ability to calculate, quantify, consider propositions and hypotheses, and carry out complete mathematical procedures. So if you consider yourself to be a logical learner, use the techniques that enable you to perceive relationships and connections using abstract, symbolic thought, sequential reasoning skills, and inductive and deductive thinking patterns. The person with logical intelligence as a talent is inclined to think more conceptually and abstractly than others and is more likely to see patterns and relationships that others will often miss. A logical/mathematical learner is very systematic and organized, and loves the challenge of a complex problem to solve. We use our logical intelligence when we recognize abstract patterns, such as counting by twos, multiplying by threes, or knowing if you've received the correct change back when you purchase something using cash. They are drawn to arithmetic problems, strategy games and experiments. Logical/mathematical learners can engage in a wide range of skills, including:

- conducting experiments;

- solving puzzles;

- asking cosmic questions;

- analyzing circumstances and people's behavior;

- working with numbers and formulas;

- creating codes, classifications and categorizations.[lxvii]

Here's a list of scientists, mathematicians, and inventors who used logic and reason to find fame and fortune—well, at least fame! Each of them also lived with a disability. Their unique combination of intelligences—strengths as well as weaknesses—made them such successful people.[lxviii]

- **Albert Einstein** was an American physicist most famous for his theory of relativity. Einstein had learning disabilities and did very poorly in school.

- **Stephen Hawking** is a British physicist noted for his study of cosmology and the big bang theory. He is also the author of the popular *A Brief History of Time*. He has an extreme physical disability and communicates with the aid of a computer.

- **Thomas Edison** was an American inventor—one of the greatest and most productive of his time. He spent only three months of his entire life in school. He was hearing impaired and may have been dyslexic.

- **Johnannes Kepler** was a 17th Century German astronomer and mathematician. Kepler's Laws describe the revolutions of planets around the sun. He was sight impaired.

- **Bill Gates** is the famed founder of Microsoft and one of the wealthiest people in the United States. He has dyslexia.

Career matches include:

- scientist

- mathematician

- lawyer/attorney

- doctor

- accountant

- bookkeeper

- computer programmer

- researcher

- financial planner

People with a strong logical intelligence usually:[lxix]

- seek order;

- reason scientifically;

- identify relationships;

- enjoy testing theories;

- like completing puzzles;

- excel at calculating numbers;

- solve problems instinctively;

- analyze abstract ideas;

- manipulate functions;

- perform mathematical operations at a rapid rate.

Bodily/Kinesthetic Talent: Good at Action, Movement, and Sports

Bodily/kinesthetic intelligence is considered the most controversial of Gardner's multiple intelligences because some researchers believe that this type of intelligence is not important. For example, as compared to the linguistic and logical intelligence, bodily kinesthetic intelligence may be downplayed in the classroom because it can be seen as a disruption to the educational process.[lxx] Gardner described bodily kinesthetic intelligence as the ability to control body movements, and to handle objects skillfully through a variety of physical skills. I see this intelligence as using the body to express emotion, to play a sport, or to create a new invention. I believe this is why "learning by doing" came into existence. This intelligence also includes a sense of timing, hand-eye coordination, and perfecting the skills of mind-body motion. People who are generally good at physical activities often prefer learning through activities, which require them to get up and move around. This means they often learn best from doing something rather than reading or hearing about it. The common characteristics of the bodily kinesthetic learner include those who:[lxxi]

- learn by doing;
- would rather touch than just look;
- are well-coordinated with good motor skills;
- like figuring out how things work;
- enjoy the outdoors;
- like to work with their hands;
- can't sit still for too long;
- enjoy sports and exhilarating experiences;
- have a lot of physical energy;
- are athletic.

Here's a list of artists, athletes, and actors whose physical intelligence propelled them into the limelight. They also happened to live with a disability.

Their unique combination of intelligences—strengths as well as weaknesses—made them such successful people.[lxxii]

- **Auguste Rodin** was a French sculptor. His most famous work is *The Thinker*. He had a learning disability.

- **Admiral Peary** was an American arctic explorer and naval officer. In addition to having strong spatial skills, he also had a strong kinesthetic intelligence. He had a communicative disorder which caused a learning disability.

- **Vaslav Nijinsky** was a Russian ballet dancer and choreographer. He was mentally ill.

- **Tom Cruise** is a Hollywood super-star. He's severely dyslexic, but he's able to memorize lines. Therefore, he's weaker in linguistics but stronger in bodily intelligence.

- **Jim Abbott** was an American baseball pitcher. He was born without a right hand.

- **Marlee Matlin** is a film and stage actress. She won the Academy Award for her role in *Children of a Lesser God*. She is hearing impaired.

Career matches include:

- athlete
- dancer
- mechanic
- performer
- craftsman
- gardener
- physical therapist

- carpenter

- builder

- firefighter

- paramedic

People with a strong kinesthetic intelligence usually:[lxxiii]

- seek to interact with their environment;

- enjoy hands-on activities;

- can remain focused on a hands-on task for an extended period of time;

- may demonstrate strong fine and/or gross motor ability;

- prefer learning centers to seat work;

- seek out other students who are physically gregarious;

- can master a principle once they can manipulate materials that demonstrate the concept;

- enjoy group games and active learning tasks;

- are different from children who are hyperactive

Figure 3. Nine forms of intelligence

Musical/Rhythmic Talent: Good with Music, Tone, and Rhythm

Gardner defines musical intelligence as the capacity to discern pitch, rhythm, timbre, and tone. This intelligence enables us to recognize, create, reproduce, and reflect on music, as demonstrated by composers, conductors, musicians, vocalists, and sensitive listeners. Interestingly, there is often an affective connection between music and the emotions; and mathematical and musical intelligences may share common thinking processes. Young adults with this kind of intelligence usually sing or hum to themselves. They are usually quite aware of sounds others may miss. This intelligence is also labeled as sound intelligence, sound smart, and musical-rhythmic intelligence. Individuals who are classified as having musical intelligence learn primarily through what can be heard with their ears and vibrations that can be felt. It is not limited to music and one does not have to be particularly rhythmic to be part of this intelligence. The common behaviors of musical learners are sometimes linked to:[lxxiv]

- rhyming

- composing

- singing

- conducting

- creating

- humming

- whistling

- rapping

- recording

- tapping

Here's a list of performers and composers who hit some high notes in their careers. Each of them also happened to live with a disability. Their unique combination of intelligences—strengths as well as weaknesses—made them such successful people.

- **Cher** is a pop star and Academy Award-winning actress. You know she's an outrageous dresser, but did you know she's dyslexic? Cher is stronger in the music intelligence, but could possibly be weaker in the linguistic intelligence.

- **Sergei Rachmaninoff** was a Russian pianist, composer, and conductor. He had a learning disability.

- **Robert Schumann** was a German composer and music critic. A hand injury forced him to abandon a career as a pianist. He had a mental illness.

- **Itzhak Perlman** was a celebrated Israeli violinist. He contracted polio as a child.

- **Ludwig van Beethoven** was a revolutionary German composer who lost his hearing as an adult. Though he could no longer perform, he continued to compose works of great depth and complexity.

- **Stevie Wonder** is an award-winning singer, composer, producer, arranger, and instrumentalist. He signed his first record deal at age 10. He has been blind since birth.

Career matches include:

- musician

- singer

- conductor

- composer

- songwriter

- music teacher

- music director

- choir director

- record producer

People with a strong rhythmic intelligence usually:[lxxv]

- seek patterns in new information;

- find patterns in their environment;

- are particularly drawn to sound;

- respond to cadence in language;

- enjoy moving to rhythms;

- pick up terms and phrases in foreign languages easily;

- use patterning to both internalize and recall skills, ideas, and concepts.

Interpersonal/Working with People Talent: Good at Communicating with Others

Interpersonal intelligence is the ability to understand and interact effectively with others. It involves effective verbal and nonverbal communication, the ability to note distinctions among the personalities of others, sensitivity to the moods and temperaments of others, and the ability to entertain multiple perspectives. Other characteristics include reacting appropriately to the needs of others and knowing how to communicate effectively and have empathy. They learn best through interaction and dialogue with other people. Young adults with this kind of intelligence are leaders among their peers, are good at communicating, and seem to understand others' feelings and motives.

Here's a list of famous individuals who were successful with the interpersonal intelligence by interaction and dialogue with other people.

- **Franklin Delano Roosevelt** was the thirty-second president of the United States. He served for twelve years, completing almost four full terms, and was the only president ever to serve more than eight years. He was stricken with a severe attack of poliomyelitis (polio), which resulted in total paralysis of both legs to the hips. Roosevelt's strengths were with interpersonal intelligence but he was weaker with bodily intelligence. Even though the bodily intelligence was his weaker one, he didn't let that stop him as he found creative ways to travel across the country while serving as the president.

- **Dr. Martin Luther King Jr.** was an American clergyman, activist, humanitarian, and leader in the Civil Rights Movement. He is best known for his role in the advancement of civil rights using nonviolent civil disobedience. He used his oratory skills to have success with the interpersonal intelligence. His speeches still make an impact on the world today in Disability Rights Movement.

- **Norman Schwarzkopf** is a Vietnam War veteran, former commander of the U.S. Central Command, and a four-star general in the US Army. After serving in Vietnam, he was plagued by cracked vertebras, which led to a major back surgery, but he didn't let that put a stop to his military career. Schwarzkopf's strength is interpersonal but he could be weaker with the bodily intelligence.

Career matches include:

- teacher /counselor

- social worker

- psychologist

- philosopher

- sales clerk

- politician

People with strong interpersonal intelligence usually:

- value relationships;

- seek the support of a group;

- solicit input from others;

- enjoy sharing things about themselves or their life experiences;

- love to see other people learn things about themselves.

Intrapersonal/Self Talent: Good at Self-Reflection

Intrapersonal intelligence is the capacity to understand oneself and one's thoughts and feelings, and to use such knowledge in planning and directing one's life. Intrapersonal intelligence involves not only an appreciation of the self, but also of the human condition. People with intrapersonal intelligence are adept at looking inward and figuring out their own feelings, motivations and goals. They are highly introspective, seek understanding, are intuitive, usually introverted, and they learn best independently. As young adults, they may be shy, highly self-motivated and they are usually unaware of their own feelings, but they tend to change as they age. Here's a list of some great thinkers and leaders who also happened to live with a disability. Their unique combination of intelligences—strengths as well as weaknesses— made them such successful people.[lxxvi]

- **Helen Keller** was an American author, lecturer, and humanitarian who was blind, deaf, and mute. Her life story and writings continue to inspire people from all walks of life.

- **General George Patton** was a brilliant American military strategist who served in both World Wars and was dyslexic.

- **Friedrich Nietzsche** was a German philosopher whose theories had a widespread influence on social, political, and cultural movements throughout the 19th and 20th centuries. He had a behavioral disorder known as Obsessive Compulsive Disorder and Obsessive Compulsive Personality Disorder.

- **Aldous Huxley** was a British writer and social critic best known for his visionary, futuristic novel *Brave New World*. Huxley was sight impaired.

- **Aristotle** was an eloquent Greek philosopher who studied under Plato and had a profound influence on western thought. Aristotle was a brilliant orator and thinker who also had a communicative disorder called bipolar.

Career matches include:

- psychologist
- philosopher
- writer
- theologian

People with a strong intrapersonal intelligence usually:[lxxvii]

- are comfortable with themselves;
- express strong likes or dislikes of particular activities;
- communicate their feelings well;

- sense their own strengths and weaknesses;

- show confidence in their abilities;

- set realistic goals;

- make appropriate choices;

- follow their instincts;

- express a sense of justice and fairness;

- relate to others based on their sense of self.

Naturalistic/Nature Talent: Good at Appreciating the World and Nature

According to Gardner, the naturalist intelligence has to do with how we relate to our surroundings and where we fit into it. People with naturalist intelligence have a sensitivity to and appreciation of nature. They are gifted at nurturing and growing things as well as caring for and interacting with animals. They can easily distinguish patterns in nature. They would rather be working out in the woods, hiking, or collecting rocks than being inside. However, if they are inside studying plants, animals, insects, living systems, or natural formations, then their motivation is more likely to soar.

Here's a list of visionary thinkers whose exploration of the natural world led to many inventions and insights, which continue to enrich our lives. Each lived with a disability. Their unique combination of intelligences—strengths as well as weaknesses—made them such successful people.[lxxviii]

- **Jules Verne** incorporated his passion for geography into his writing. His extraordinary view of the world continues to capture our imagination. His works include *A Journey to the Center of the Earth* and *Twenty Thousand Leagues Under the Sea*. Verne is believed to have had attention deficit disorder (ADD).

- **Louis Pasteur** was a French chemist whose discoveries in the late 1800s include the process of pasteurization and the rabies vaccine. Pasteur's scientific insights helped make the world a safer place. He had ADD.

- **Henry David Thoreau** was an American author and naturalist who depicted the beauty of the world through his poetry and essays. This brilliant writer had ADD. Thoreau's experiences living in a cabin on Walden Pond inspired his masterpiece, *Walden.*

Career matches include:

- conservationist
- gardener
- farmer
- animal trainer
- park ranger
- scientist
- botanist
- zookeeper
- geologist
- marine biologist
- ecologist
- veterinarian

People with a strong naturalist intelligence usually:[lxxix]

- are intrinsically organized;
- demonstrate an empathy with nature;

- pick up on subtle differences in meaning;

- like to make collections of materials;

- enjoy sorting and organizing materials;

- impose their own sense of order on new information;

- respond to semantic mapping activities;

- prefer charts, tables, diagrams, and timelines.

Existential/Spiritual Talent: Good at Defining the Meaning of Life.

According to Gardner, the existential intelligence is concerned with the ability to be sensitive by trying to understand and tackle deep questions about human existence, such as the meaning of life, why we are born and why we die, and how we got here.

Here's a couple of famous individuals who used the existential intelligence in order to answer the deepest questions about life.

- **Socrates** was a classical Greek philosopher. He's been credited as one of the founders of Western philosophy. He is an enigmatic figure known chiefly through the accounts of later classical writers, especially the writings of his students, Plato and Xenophon.[lxxx]

- **Thomas Dexter Jakes**, better known as T.D. Jakes is the bishop/chief pastor of The Potter's House, a non-denominational American mega church with thirty thousand members.[lxxxi] He went from being a young child with a speech impediment to being one of the foremost Christian speakers in the world. He is utilizing his strength in the existential intelligence to change the world even though his weaker area is possibly the linguistic intelligence.

Gardner defines the core of existential intelligence as twofold:

1. To locate oneself with respect to the furthest reaches of the cosmos—the infinite no less than the infinitesimal, and

2. To locate oneself with respect to the existential features of the human condition—the significance of life, the meaning of death, the ultimate fate of the physical and psychological worlds, and such profound experiences as love of another human being, or total immersion in a work of art.[lxxxii]

People with a strong existential intelligence usually:[lxxxiii]

- seek meaningful learning;

- like to synthesize ideas based on their learning;

- enjoy literature and customs from other cultures;

- have a strong connection with family and friends;

- develop a strong identity with their neighborhood and town;

- express a sense of belonging to a global community;

- like to get involved with social and political causes;

- can have a strong commitment to their health and well-being;

- tend to look at information relative to the context in which it is presented.

Career matches include:

- scientist

- philosopher

- theologian

- spiritual leader

I've learned that the good news surrounding these nine intelligences defined by Gardner is that you and I possess all of these talents! However, we're likely to have more strength in some areas than others, and in some areas we might have some limitations. But the point is, we need to take the time to discover and value the talents we have and use them to serve God, our communities, and our families. And based on the successful examples mentioned for each talent, consider how they were able to not only overcome their weaknesses, but the fact that they focused on their strengths because that is what helped them to identify their talents.

The Parable of Talents

The purpose of the intelligence discussion is that once you've recognized your strengths, you can be incredibly successful despite your weaknesses. Sometimes when recognizing a weakness, we have a tendency to lose sight of our strengths, especially when faced with a new challenge (like identifying and living our purpose). But once we can identify where our talents lie, our strengths will begin to shine. And when our strengths begin to shine, we will be able to overcome any weakness because we have something that will keep us focused on our talents. So the next time you think about your talents, remember this story of the parable of talents that Jesus shared with his disciples in Matthew 25:14–30. (NKJV)

> *For the kingdom of heaven is like a man traveling to a far country, who called his own servants and delivered his goods to them. And to one he gave five talents, to another two, and to another one, to each according to his own ability; and immediately he went on a journey. Then he who had received the five talents went and traded with them, and made another five talents. And likewise he who had received two gained two more also. But he who had received one went and dug in the ground, and hid his Lord's money. After a long time the Lord of those servants came and settled accounts with*

them. So he who had received five talents came and brought five other talents, saying, "Lord, you delivered to me five talents; look, I have gained five more talents besides them." His Lord said to him, "Well done, good and faithful servant; you were faithful over a few things, I will make you ruler over many things. Enter into the joy of your Lord." He also who had received two talents came and said, "Lord, you delivered to me two talents; look, I have gained two more talents besides them." His Lord said to him, "Well done, good and faithful servant; you have been faithful over a few things, I will make you ruler over many things. Enter into the joy of your Lord." Then he who had received the one talent came and said, "Lord, I knew you to be a hard man, reaping where you have not sown, and gathering where you have not scattered seed. And I was afraid, and went and hid your talent in the ground. Look, there you have what is yours." But his Lord answered and said to him, "You wicked and lazy servant, you knew that I reap where I have not sown, and gather where I have not scattered seed. So you ought to have deposited my money with the bankers, and at my coming I would have received back my own with interest. Therefore take the talent from him, and give it to him who has ten talents. For to everyone who has, more will be given, and he will have abundance; but from him who does not have, even what he has will be taken away. And cast the unprofitable servant into the outer darkness. There will be weeping and gnashing of teeth."

Jesus shared this parable to encourage them in their time of waiting for his return as to what a servant should be doing. And believers are like these servants who are also awaiting the return of their master, and this story has some lessons for us about what we should be doing with our talents in the meantime. This parable leaves us with four principles, which should encourage us to discover our talents so our purpose can be built on a solid foundation. I believe these four principles will help you to keep your purpose as your main focus.

Principle 1—What We Have is Not Our Own (v. 14)

Like the scripture says, we are on a journey called life, and we are called to be God's servants who are entrusted with his property. The property that we have been given are the talents that God has blessed us with. We are also told in Psalm 24:1 (KJV), "The earth is the Lord's, and all its fullness, the world and those who dwell therein." So everything on the earth already belongs to God, and we are to use the talents he's given us to glorify God and to serve the common good of humanity. When you recognize that what you have is not yours, you'll be more apt to accept that success is the product of work.

Principle 2—We Are Given All That We Can Handle (v.15)

Of course, some have more talents than others as described in the scripture. According to the fifteenth verse, each servant was given a particular number of talents based on their ability. This is where most people began to complain because someone else had been given more. When some people have less than others, they tend to want people to feel sorry for them. But what if that one talent described in these scriptures was valued at a million dollars? The person with the one talent would have been given more than enough the meet the master's expectations. This point should help us to recognize that our job is to make the most of what we've been given. Are you trying to passively preserve what's been entrusted to you or are you trying to generate a return on your talents? Be the best you that you can be. As author Robin Sharma insisted, "Investing in yourself is the best investment you will ever make. For it will not only improve your life, it will improve the lives of all those around you."[lxxxiv] As you make an investment in the talents God has given you, you'll know that you're making the world a better place because you've been able to take care of what you've been blessed with.

Principle 3—We Will Be Accountable For What
We Do With What We Have (vv. 16–19)

This is where the story begins to separate the believers from the doubters. All of the servants did something with what they were given, but the difference lies in what they each did with what was given to them. The first two servants immediately went to work by investing what they had, and they each generated a double return on their master's investment. The first two servants had faith by taking a risk with what they had. The third servant was scared and did not believe, so he buried his talent only to have it taken away when his master returned. Probably one of the most overlooked points of this parable is the fact that God gave each servant talents according to their ability. I believe that God understands that some of us are not capable of producing what others can produce. I don't believe this is unfair, but I do believe that this is where diversity is woven into the parable. Since we're all different and we all have diverse gifts and talents, it would be wise to use what we have. As author George Martin maintained, "Different roads sometimes lead to the same castle."[lxxxv] So let us all be accountable for what we have been given.

Principle 4—What We Do with What We Have Been Given
Reveals Our View of God (vv. 20–25)

Each of the first two servants received the master's praise, "Well done, good and faithful servant." I believe that every believer wants to hear Jesus say, "Well done," but I don't think Jesus will say so unless we have done well. And the best way to do well is to believe in Jesus and have faith in using the talents that you've been given. Jesus also told the first two servants, "I will make you a ruler," and both servants were invited to "enter into the joy of the Lord." As for the last servant, he definitely didn't hear the words "well done," and he was very fearful because he knew he didn't do what he was supposed to do. As for his master making him a promise, that didn't happen either. Actually, everything he had was taken away from him because he was lazy and he was only thinking of himself. When we only think of ourselves, we're not taking on the view of who God is in our lives. We must not make excuses to avoid what God calls us and equips us to do. For if we avoid what God has called us to do, then everything that we've been given will be taken away.

The moral of the parable and the insight into the nine talents described by Gardner is to make use of the talents that you have, and you will be rewarded in abundance; but if you neglect to nurture your gifts then the little that you have will be taken away. But more importantly, you'll never be able to discover your life's purpose. And the best way to do that is to make use of your gifts by growing them through constant practice. As I shared earlier, everyone has some form of the nine talents, but it's up to you to figure out which one best fits your skill set. Get out there and discover what your passion is. When you put a limit on what you will do, you're putting a limit on what you can do. As pianist, conductor and composer André George Previn maintained, "If I miss a day of practice, I know it. If I miss two days, my manager knows it. If I miss three days, my audience knows it."[lxxxvi] Hence, as long as you live, don't miss a day of practice living your purpose because not only has it been discovered, but you are the proof that you have the emotional, physiological, and spiritual ability to do it. And the fact that you've read this chapter means that you have the intelligence to do it.

Chapter 4
Define Your Purpose

I will never let someone else's opinion define my reality.

—*Steve Maraboli*

THINK ABOUT BEING on vacation at your favorite location. Is it the beach? Is it the mountains? Wherever it is, you're probably going to spend money on food, drinks, gas, clothing, and other items. And if you think about it, you're a customer to several different types of businesses. Have you ever thought about why you spend your money with a particular business and not another? I can tell you why. It's because name brand recognition gives us the feeling of security their services or products provide. We are more likely to purchase a product or service from a company that makes us feel more comfortable. As discussed in the previous chapter, market researchers have discovered customers make purchasing decisions based on one factor: whichever business, brand, or specific product comes to mind first. So how do businesses get their brand to catapult to the top of our subconscious? Marketing professionals call it TOMA or top of mind awareness. It's also a way to measure how well brands rank in the minds of their consumers.

A perfect example of this is discussed in a *Forbes* magazine article titled "Define Your Brand's Purpose, Not Just Its Promise." Allen Adamson insisted that in a marketplace in which consumer confidence is low and budgetary vigilance is high, what separates the businesses is not just the promise made about their products, but that those businesses have a defined purpose. The article also shares some insight into the Wal-Mart story as to how the "low prices" slogan was seen as a liability by the media and some consumers. According to Stephen Quinn, Chief Marketing Officer of Wal-Mart, management recognized that the promise was as good as empty without its purpose as support. Adamson stated that company leaders, seeking guidance, looked back to the original intent of founder Sam Walton's promise of offering lower prices to help people provide better lives for their families. Quinn emphasized that building a brand on a purpose isn't just to help consumers, but it's also to help guide employees and associates in understanding why "we are here."[lxxxvii] This awareness about building a brand on purpose shows how people's lives can be affected by organizations that have a defined the purpose. Even with Wal-Mart's success of a defined purpose, there is still much work to be done in the arena of customer service and employee relations. Adrian Campos writes in an article titled "Why Costco is beating Wal-Mart" that Costco is always changing its brand and introducing new products in order to provide customers with a pleasant "treasure hunt" experience.[lxxxviii] And according to a Forbes article by Rick Ungar, Costco pays their employees a livable wage and gets sales per employee at double what Wal-Mart subsidiary Sam's Club gets from their employee who work for lesser pay.[lxxxix] Needless to say, even though their purpose is defined, Wal-Mart has a lot of work to do.

As you can see with the Wal-Mart and Costco example, purpose can be defined for any organization, large or small. And if purpose can be defined for an organization as big as Wal-Mart, surely purpose can be defined for individuals who want to make a difference in their own life and in the lives of others. In order for individuals to define their purpose, I suggest beginning by applying discipline in several major areas. I've been able to apply discipline in these areas, which has helped me, and they are the foundation on which my purpose has been defined. I've been able to define my purpose by being **disciplined with my thinking, by taking risks, and by challenging my own B.S. (belief system)**. Before we delve into these areas, I would like to define and discuss the art of discipline; without it, these components will not stand the test when challenged.

Discipline

Perhaps the most valuable result of all education is the ability to make yourself do the thing you have to do, whether you like it or not.
—*Thomas Henry Huxley*

According to the Merriam-Webster dictionary, discipline is defined as the practice of training to observe a code of behavior for self-control.[x] I define discipline as doing what needs to be done, when it needs to be done, in the best possible way every time it needs to be done. And as a result, no discipline plus no motivation equals a lack of self-appreciation. I've learned that self-discipline leads to self-motivation and a lack of self-motivation is the result of a lack of self-appreciation. In the book, *Living Deeply*, the authors share their discovery that all life-changing decisions have what they call the "four essential elements of transformative practice," which I relate to discipline. These elements are crucial for anyone considering disciplining themselves in any phase of their life. The four elements are intention, attention, repetition, and guidance.[xci]

The first element the authors discuss is the art of intention. In order to be disciplined in anything, we would have to be intentional about the choices that are made at every opportunity. Comedian Norman MacDonald joked, "Do not imagine that the good you intend will balance the evil you perform."[xcii] But all humor aside, good intentions will not help us on our way if we take the wrong road. With every choice we make, whether good or bad, we enter those choices knowing that we have intentions for the outcome of the choice to play a role in our life. When we have a disciplined intention, we feel more like an active participant in making ourselves better. When we are force to do something we didn't want to do, the intention is not the same. If we do not actively change our intentions, then our choices will not change. And when our choices don't change, we don't have the discipline to change ourselves.

The second element discussed by the authors is the art of attention. Attention can be defined as notice taken of someone or something. In order for us to have discipline in anything, we have to pay close attention to things that we may have never noticed before such as how we're spending our time, who we're spending our time with, and where we spend our resources. Author of *Switch: How to Change When things is Hard*, Chip Heath maintains that the most basic way to get someone's attention is to break a pattern. Have you ever paid attention to the patterns in your daily life? What about the pattern of your daily activities? Or better yet, the patterns of what you do when you get home every day? If you pay close attention, you'll be delighted to see new things, which you might currently be taking for granted. There is no way we can create discipline in our life without paying attention to what has our attention. If we are preoccupied with trying to prove something to others, then we'll need those people's attention to be able to prove it. And at the end of the day, we won't have the discipline of our own attention, which it needs in order to focus on the important personal things in life because we're focusing on aspects of the lives of other people.

The third element shared by the authors is the art of repetition. Repetition is the act of repeating something that has already been written, said, or done. History has a way of repeating itself, and if we aren't paying attention, we will be in a constant cycle of repetition. If we have the knowledge, the wisdom, and the understanding of the past, we will be able to break the old cycle and begin a new and improved pattern. I've learned that whenever I discover a truth to act as if I'm telling it to a parrot; for every truth that we're exposed to needs constant repetition. Therefore, whatever we want to do right, we must constantly do it over and over again. And when this process is constantly repeated, the act then becomes second nature, and it becomes a part of who we are.

The last element shared by the authors is the art of guidance. Anytime we want to do something new and different, we'll need some guidance to show us the way when we may not be getting our desired results. There's an old fable that says, "When the student is ready, the teacher appears." One key point to know is that all guidance is not an external factor. Many people believe that guidance comes from outside sources, and in some cases that might be true. But for the sake of disciplining yourself to define your purpose, your guidance must come from within. We're all born with an inner knowing power that guides us through life. We must know that God has designed humans to listen so that voice can guide us. I've learned to not entrust my future into the hands of someone else who might simply have an opinion or just some good advice on the choices I should make. Don't get me wrong, it's good to have a mentor or someone we can talk to, but we must never replace our internal composite nature of trusting God with someone else's voice. I've learned to trust that God's guidance will always lead me to where he wants. So, be disciplined with your guidance and never let go.

When all four of these elements (intention, attention, repetition, and guidance) are combined on a consistent basis, discipline will be sustained and we will be driven by inspiration and engaged by a revised desire and discipline to be the best person possible. And once we're on the highway of life driven by inspiration to be the best we can, the definition of our purpose will be clear. Then our life will be like the statue of *David*, the famous work by Italian sculptor, painter, architect, and poet Michelangelo. This statue is one of the world's most recognizable statues because it is a raw representation of the biblical King David of the Old Testament. Michelangelo was quoted saying, "In every block of marble I see a statue as plain as though it stood before me, shaped and perfect in attitude and action. I have only to hew away the rough walls that imprison the lovely apparition to reveal it to other eyes as mine see it." I am sure that while Michelangelo was sculpting the statue, others only saw a rock. Just like Michelangelo creating the statue of *David*, it's up to us to define and shape our purpose in life. And when we are done, we should have something to leave behind for others to see as we do.

Thinking

The eye sees only what the mind is prepared to comprehend.
—*Henri Bergson*

Have you ever thought about what you think about? I have. And I realized that I need to change my thoughts in order to change my reality. Essayist, lecturer, and poet Ralph Waldo Emerson maintained that we become what we think about all day long, and that nothing is sacred but the integrity of your own mind. In my pursuit to define my purpose, one of the first things I realized that I needed to do was to analyze my thinking. Also in my pursuit to define my purpose, I realized that I needed to examine how other successful people think, which has helped me to analyze my own thinking.

Merriam-Webster defines thinking as the action of using your mind to produce ideas, decisions and memories. Based on my life experiences, I define thinking as my mind talking to my soul and my soul talking to my mind. Probably one of the best definitions for thinking comes from the Bible in the book of Romans 12:2, "And be not conformed to this world, but be ye transformed by the renewing of your mind, that ye may prove what *is* that good, and acceptable, and perfect will of God." (KJV) All of these definitions indicate that we must use our thinking to truly define what we want in life and to define what God's will is for our life. Accordingly, if we want our purpose to become defined, we have to think differently about what society or the world is offering us in thought. If what is offered doesn't add up to who we are, then we need to activate a thorough thought process to define what we should and should not think. So we must challenge our own thinking in order to create our purpose and to define it more clearly.

A great example of someone having to challenge their own thinking to define their purpose is record producer and songwriter Berry Gordy. He is best known as the founder of the Motown record label. His story is legendary. With an $800 loan, he formed his own music company after a chance meeting with aspiring artist William "Smokey" Robinson, who formed The

Miracles. Motown released The Miracles' song, "Shop Around," which was written and led by Robinson, and it sold more than a million copies. This also helped to launch other aspiring artists such as Diana Ross and The Supremes, The Temptations, The Four Tops, Stevie Wonder, Marvin Gaye, Gladys Knight and The Pips, and many others.[xciii]

Gordy grew up in a large family, and he was the seventh of eight children. At the age of five, he took classical piano lessons from his uncle. And as a teenager and young adult, he worked in his father's small construction company. He later worked at the Ford Motor Company on an assembly line and then did a small stint in the army. After failure with his initial foray into the music business with a record store, he began writing songs for local rhythm and blues acts. And this is where he eventually got his big break. Gordy insisted that it was his thinking that carried him through all the failure that he endured, which enabled his breakthrough into the music industry. He said, "Don't judge yourself by other's standards ... have your own. And don't get caught up into the trap of changing yourself to fit the world. The world has to change to fit you. And if you stick to your principles, values, and morals long enough, it will. We stuck to who we were at Motown, and the world eventually came around."[xciv]

Even now, the Motown sound and music is constantly transferring from generation to generation. It's cool to see my nieces and nephews sing and dance to songs like "Sugar Pie, Honey Bunch" by The Four Tops, or "My Girl" by The Temptations, or "Baby Love" by the Supremes, and my personal favorites, "ABC" and "I Want You Back" by The Jackson 5. Having the right frame of mind is what allowed Gordy to envision a process in which an unknown performer could walk in off the street and come out a polished artist. Gordy insisted that there weren't enough people who cared about the future because they were too busy worrying about today and what they could immediately grab. I'm glad that Gordy was thinking about the future because future generations and I will be able to enjoy the musical ingenuity and spirit of soul music.

Another great example of someone having to challenge their own thinking was Cassius Clay, who is better known as Muhammad Ali. I consider Ali to be the greatest heavyweight boxer in sports history. And based on his success and his flamboyant personality, one would be shocked to think that Ali had to challenge his thinking. Growing up as Cassius Clay in Louisville, Kentucky, he had an experience that led him to pursue the sport of boxing. During the Louisville Home Show, he had his bicycle stolen. Clay eventually found Joe Martin, a Louisville police officer, and told him that he wanted to "whip" whoever stole his bicycle. In his spare time, Martin would train young boxers at a local Louisville gym. Martin told Ali, "Well, you better learn how to fight before you start challenging people that you gonna whip." Martin would encourage the young Cassius Clay to channel his anger and intensity into something positive that would help ease his frustration over his bike. Martin began training the young Clay, and he soon made his amateur ring debut—a three-minute, three-round split decision with Ronnie O'Keefe. The future world heavyweight champion earned four dollars for his first fight. Martin was quoted as saying, "He stood out because he had more determination than most boys. He was a kid willing to make the sacrifices necessary to achieve something worthwhile in sports. It was almost impossible to discourage him. He was easily the hardest worker of any kid I ever taught."[xcv] For the next twenty-seven years, Ali would not only be in the ring, but he would dominate in the ring with a record of fifty-six wins (thirty-seven knockouts, nineteen decisions), five losses (four decisions, one retirement).[xcvi] Those who might not know or understand the personality of Ali might believe that he was cocky or arrogant, but based on what I've learned about him, he was constantly training his own thoughts to be confident that he was the greatest boxer ever. And based on all of his accomplishments, he is considered to be the greatest by boxing fans. Below are ten of my all-time favorite quotes from The Greatest (as Ali referred to himself):

- "I hated every minute of training, but I said, 'Don't quit. Suffer now and live the rest of your life as a champion.'"

- "Champions aren't made in gyms. Champions are made from something they have deep inside them—a desire, a dream, and a vision. They have to have the skill and the will. But the will must be stronger than the skill."

- "Live everyday as if it were your last because someday you're going to be right."

- "The best way to make your dreams come true is to wake up."

- "You lose nothing when fighting for a cause ... In my mind the losers are those who don't have a cause they care about."

- "Often it isn't the mountains ahead that wear you out, it's the little pebble in your shoe."

- "If they can make penicillin out of moldy bread, then they can sure make something out of you."

- "He who is not courageous enough to take risks will accomplish nothing in life."

- "If you even dream of beating me, you'd better wake up and apologize."

- "It's hard to be humble, when you're as great as I am."

As you can see from his own words, Ali had an eccentric personality that was larger than life. Those who thought he was cocky and arrogant really couldn't appreciate his desire to become the best boxer in the world. So whether you like or dislike him, has this information changed your thoughts about him? Or better yet, has his story changed your insight about defining your purpose? His story should encourage you to change your thinking about what's possible for yourself.

I've been able to do a lot of different things all by just changing my thinking. By changing my thinking, I've been able to get a bachelor's degree, a master's degree, a doctoral degree, and author my first couple of books. And probably one of the biggest results of changing my thinking is that now I have the confidence I need to pursue my goal and dream of owning my own business as a professional speaker and consultant. My current passions and desires remind me of physician, poet, professor, lecturer, and author Oliver Wendell Holmes, Sr. He stated, "Once a person's mind has been expanded on a thought, an idea or a concept, it can never be satisfied to going back to the way it was."[xcvii] Based on the fact that I've expanded my thinking on the thought, idea, and concept of defining my purpose in life, I know that I can never be satisfied to going back to the way it was when I didn't know my purpose, or to when I didn't have the confidence to stand boldly before audiences to share my personal story of triumph, or to when I didn't have the courage to stand alone and apart from the crowd to listen to the small voice of God telling me to pursue the call on my life, or to when I didn't have the courage to do the right thing when the wrong thing was presented before me. I'm learning more and more each day that everything matters, even the small things, just by expanding my thought process. I'll share these thoughts with you, which I call "Everything matters."

One alphabet leads to a word,

One word leads to a sentence,

One sentence leads to a paragraph,

One paragraph leads to a chapter,

One chapter leads to a book,

One book leads to a story,

One story leads to a thought,

One thought leads to an idea,

One idea leads to action,

One action leads to a habit,

One habit leads to a lifestyle,

One lifestyle leads to a legacy,

One legacy leads to everything.

So as you contemplate how you can evaluate your thought process, just know that everything matters. In my pursuit to define my purpose, I've not only read about other successful people, but I've been able to learn how they think. A lot of times, I get caught up in the lessons of the actions of successful people, but now I've learned to examine what goes on in their heads—particularly the way they think. I think it's important because we have to make decisions even when we have conflicting ideas in mind. I believe that anyone who considers himself or herself to be successful has learned how to think through conflicting ideas as well as how to base actions on the most desirable outcome.

In the article "How Successful Leaders Think," Roger Martin describes how the secret to becoming a great leader is not to act like one but to think like one. Martin explains that successful and brilliant leaders excel at integrative thinking because they can hold two opposing ideas in their minds at once, and then rather than settling for choice A or B, they're able to forge a creative "third way" that contains elements of both A and B, which improves each of them.[xcviii] Integrative thinking uses all available information in order to make the best decision possible. Can you see that in the two examples of Barry Gordy and Mohammad Ali? Both were able to become integrative thinkers instead of conventional "either-or" thinkers, and they were able to embrace their options by seeking solutions when they made their decisions.

I use the four stages in the decision making process whenever I'm making a decision, especially when it comes to defining my purpose. And I believe that in order for you to use your thinking as a tool to define your purpose, you must go through the process described by Martin. This process has helped me grow from a conventional thinker to an integrative thinker. According to Martin, the first stage is learning to identity key factors. This is when conventional thinkers consider only obviously relevant factors when weighing options, while integrative thinkers seek less obvious but potentially more relevant factors when weighing options. The second stage is analyzing causality. This is when conventional thinkers consider one-way linear relations between factors, and integrative thinkers consider multi-directional relationships between factors. The third stage is envisioning your decision's overall structure. This is when conventional thinkers break a problem into pieces and work on them separately, while integrative thinkers see a problem as a whole by examining how different aspects affect one another. And the last stage in the decision making process is called achieving the desired resolution. This is where conventional thinkers make either-or choices, and integrative thinkers refuse to accept the conventional options.[xcix] Integrative thinkers are more likely to use a variety of inputs to get the desired outcome.

This is important because we will need to depend on our decision making skills when we face problems and challenges along the journey to defining our purpose. I've learned that conventional thinkers seek simplicity and are often forced to make unattractive trade-offs, which normally leads to a delay in the true definition of purpose. For instance, I know my purpose is to change lives with words by speaking and writing, and I wanted a very simple and easy way to do that. A conventional way for me to do that is to post positive thoughts and statuses on my social networking pages such as Facebook, LinkedIn, and Twitter. Even though I might be fulfilling and defining my purpose, these conventional ways are really not encouraging me to stretch myself because they are too simple.

I've learned that by becoming an integrative thinker I have forced myself to stretch. It has allowed me to welcome new and different approaches to finding alternate avenues for me to define and mold my purpose because that is where I've found my best answers. Those best answers have led me to write books and to purse my professional career as a motivational speaker, trainer, and consultant. In the *Forbes* magazine article "Solving the Decisiveness Dilemma: The 4 Step Process for Making an Excellent Choice," author Joseph Folkman describes what I believe is the best process for making decisions. He explains how the decision making process tends to force us to generate a lot of assumptions, which sometimes forces us to collect too much data in order to make a basic decision. And whenever we have too much information, we can become ineffective with what is known as 'analysis paralysis.' This is when we overanalyze a situation, so that a decision or action is never taken, in effect paralyzing our outcome.[c] I believe Folkman's four step process is a great avenue to put us on the right road to making excellent choices through decision making, which should keep us from analysis paralysis. His first recommendation is to try to spot all the problems, opportunities, and trends that might affect our current decision. I believe the more problems and trends that we tend to discover means that we're more likely to make the best decision.

Folkman's second recommendation is to look for at least three possible solutions before we make the decision. Most people generally try to narrow their choices down to a single choice before making a decision. The problem with that is that we tend to be blind to our best choice because we're only looking for one. I remind myself that when I'm only looking for one solution, I am trying to be perfect; but when I'm looking for at least three solutions, I'm open to other possibilities.

Folkman's third recommendation is to go the extra mile in collecting and gathering information. He insists that a frequent problem with decision making is that people gather only the data that's quickly available and is supportive of their favorite alternative. Then they decide. But when other information is available, but is never gathered or considered, it could result in a less favorable decision.

And the last recommendation he makes is to keep inspiration as part of our arsenal. Of course, it's easy to assume that good decisions are only based on facts and data, but the human element of inspiration can favorably influence the success of the decisions we make. As you begin the decision making process in defining your purpose with your thinking, consider Folkman's four step process to help you make an excellent choice.

I hope these examples can help you on your journey as you expand your thinking to define your purpose. Just know that once you pursue those things that help you define your purpose, you will eventually attempt those things you didn't think were possible. In 1 Corinthians 2:9–10, Apostle Paul said, "Eye has not seen, nor ear heard, nor have entered into the heart of man the things which God has prepared for those who love Him. But God has revealed them to us through His Spirit. For the Spirit searches all things, yes, the deep things of God." (NKJV) So as we get our thinking in line by opening up our mind to see the possibilities, God will continue to reveal to us all the spiritual things we need to experience. And that will help us to continue to define our purpose.

Risk

Whenever we're afraid of change, we've failed to realize that we've become kings and queens of our comfort zone. Today is a good day to denounce yourself from the throne of your comfort zone because you don't put new wine into old wine skins.

—*Dr. Samuel Jones*

How would you like to be king or queen for a day? I would say that you would probably love for that to happen because you would be able to have whatever you want. You could do what you want. Or maybe you could go where you want. But what if I was to tell you that you are already a king or queen? Would you believe that? I believe that we're all kings and queens of our comfort zones because we tend to create decrees that encourage us to remain the same. On average, most people don't like change because as humans it's in our nature to want to be comfortable. But I've learned that in order to define my purpose, I must continue to take risks to stretch myself because that is the only way my gifts will be revealed. So as you ponder those thoughts, I hope this section on risk will encourage you to dethrone yourself from the throne of comfort. In exchange for being king or queen of your comfort zone, you'll end up as king or queen of your universe.

It was author Ralph Waldo Emerson who said that until you attempt to do something beyond what you've already mastered, you will never grow. So not only in terms of defining your purpose, but also in terms of growing as a person, it's important to take risks. Allow the above examples to encourage you to take the risks you need to define your purpose.

"Safety first" has always been a motto that gets attention. Whenever I see "safety first," I think "play it safe." I guess I see it that way because of my athletic background. But as I've developed more as a writer, a speaker, and a leader in my home, my church, and my community, I don't just want to play it safe. I want to become the best that I can be through my leadership and influence based on what I've learned and how I want to continue to grow as a person. I know for that to happen I must take calculated risks that will stretch my belief, my abilities, and my faith. Therefore, the person who is seeking to define their purpose and pursue their goals in life must recognize that risks must be taken. The Australian nurse who pioneered physical therapy, Elizabeth Kenny, insisted, "It is better to be a lion for a day rather than a sheep all your life."[ci] The correlation to that quote is that lions are known to take risks, and sheep are apt to not take risks. She's really saying that if you dare for nothing, you need not hope for anything. Australian novelist and playwright Morris West vowed, "If you spend your whole life waiting for the storm, you'll never enjoy the sunshine." So have you ever thought about why you don't take risks? According to the *Forbes* article, "Take a Risk: The Odds Are Better Than You Think," contributor and author Margie Warrell maintained that we normally overestimate the probability that something is going to go wrong.[cii] As Daniel Kahneman wrote in the book, *Thinking, Fast and Slow*, whenever we evaluate risk, we tend to envision or imagine that our potential losses would be greater than potential gains.[ciii] David Viscott wrote, "If your life is ever going to get better, you'll have to take risks. There is simply no way you can grow without taking chances."[civ] And I always consider the advice of one of my favorite race car drivers, Mario Andretti, when he said, "If things seem under control, then you are not going fast enough." So if you're really in control, you're not risking enough; and in reality, you're really risking everything because you're not growing.

Warrell also contended that we exaggerate the consequence of what might happen if things do go wrong. This is the "what if" phase that I was experiencing about my public speaking class back at the University of Southern Mississippi, which I shared in the previous chapter. This is what Warrell calls "catastrophizing." She insisted, "We come up with dire and dramatic worst-case scenario images in our minds-eye. Rather than assume that we would act quickly to head off or mitigate a situation if things started going off track, we imagine everything spiraling shockingly out of control while we passively stand by, conjuring up images of ourselves destitute, shunned by our family, ostracized by our peers and forever shamed by our failure." While I've learned to not exaggerate the consequences of what might go wrong, I'm exaggerating the fact that no matter what happens, it's going to work out best for me. One of many scriptures that helps me to keep this in mind whenever I'm taking a risk is found in the book of Romans 8:28 when Paul said, "And we know that all things work together for good to them that love God, to them who are called according to his purpose."[cv] (KJV) Having these thoughts on my mind make it easier to take risks.

Another point that Warrell stressed is that we underestimate our ability to handle the consequences of the risks that we take. Even though this goes hand in hand with the previous point, this mainly focuses on the personal skills to deal with whatever happens based on the risks we've taken. I challenge myself to trust that I can respond to whatever happens based on the decision I've made. I know that I can't do it on my own, so I must have help. When was the last time you underestimated yourself when faced with a risky option and made the easier choice? How did you feel after you realized that you could have performed that particular task? Did you feel like you let yourself down? We've all faced similar situations. The point is to learn from the experience so that it does not repeat itself. If you don't believe in yourself and take a risk on yourself, no one else will be inclined to take a risk on you either. The next time you're stuck in the challenge of trusting yourself with taking a risk to do something new or different than what you're accustomed to, consider the words of Robert Frost with his famous, classic poem, the "Road Not Taken"[cvi]:

Two roads diverged in a yellow wood,

And sorry I could not travel both

And be one traveller, long I stood

And looked down one as far as I could

To where it bent in the undergrowth;

Then took the other, as just as fair,

And having perhaps the better claim,

Because it was grassy and wanted wear;

Though as for that the passing there

Had worn them really about the same,

And both that morning equally lay

In leaves no step had trodden black.

Oh, I kept the first for another day!

Yet knowing how way leads on to way,

I doubted if I should ever come back.

I shall be telling this with a sigh

Somewhere ages and ages hence:

Two roads diverged in a wood, and I

I took the one less traveled by,

And that has made all the difference.

And probably the most important point that Warrell suggested is that we discount or deny the cost of inaction by failing to take a risk, and we stick with the status quo. Have you ever used the words: "It's not that bad," or "It is what it is," or "It'll take care of itself?" I can probably go on and on. And the reason why I can go on and on is because I've used those words. I've learned that using such phrases only gives me an excuse to think that my circumstances will somehow just get better over time. Essayist, publisher, and playwright T.S. Eliot contended, "Only those who risk going too far can possibly find out how far they can go."[cvii] I've learned that I need to listen to the words that I say to myself when I'm unknowingly supporting the status quo. Former Super Bowl winning Coach Jimmy Johnson passionately asked his team, "Do you want to be safe and good, or do you want to take a chance and be great?" As Warrell put in her book *Stop Playing Safe*, "We innately avert risk and we are afraid of putting our vulnerability on the line. The status quo can seem like an easier, softer, less scary option."[cviii] But I've learned that if you really want to define your purpose, you must have the courage to take the necessary risks to attempt those things you might be afraid to do. Consider these three examples to truly understand the risks they took as they lived their life on purpose.

- Colonel Sanders (businessman, best known for founding Kentucky Fried Chicken (KFC))

  Harland Sanders was a sixth-grade dropout, a farmhand, an army mule-tender, a locomotive fireman, a railroad worker, an aspiring lawyer, an insurance salesman, a ferryboat entrepreneur, a tire salesman, an amateur obstetrician, an (unsuccessful) political candidate, a gas station operator, a motel operator, and finally, a restaurateur. When Sanders was 65, a new interstate highway snatched the traffic away from his restaurant in Corbin, Kentucky, and when he retired Sanders was left with nothing but a Social Security check and a secret recipe for fried chicken.[cix] And as it turns out, this secret recipe was all he needed to take a risk and leave his mark on the world. His risk taking led him to getting on the road to sell his secret recipe to restaurant owners, who would give him a share of the sales. The first restaurateur he called on turned him down. So did the second. So did the third.

  As a matter of fact, the first 1,008 sales calls Colonel Sanders made ended in rejection. With his recipe and risk in hand, he continued to call on owners as he traveled across the USA, sleeping in his car to save money. And eventually, prospect number 1,009 gave him his first "yes," and things began to multiply from there. Today, there are more than fifteen thousand KFC outlets in 105 countries and territories around the world.[cx] I'm glad Colonel Sanders took a risk to pursue his purpose as an entrepreneur because now the world is able to enjoy the results.

Figure 4. Colonel Sanders[cxi]

- George Burns (comedian, actor, and writer)

George Burns was one of those famous personalities who lived life to the fullest, always taking risks by trying his skills in different venues. Burns first took a risk when he dropped out of school in the fourth grade to pursue show business.[cxii] During a seventy-five year career in show business, Burns explored his talents in areas that included music, television and film, radio, and even as an author. Burns was known for his off-the-cuff remarks while he puffed on his signature cigar. Until his death at the age of 100, he smoked as many as ten cigars a day.[cxiii] One of the things I most admired about him is the fact that it didn't matter how old he was, he always took the risk by trying his hand at different things. For example, at the age of 87, Burns signed a five-year contract with Caesar's World in Las Vegas, now known as Caesar's Palace. And by staying true to his comedic personality, he insisted, "I can't afford to die when I'm booked. The last time I played Caesar's Palace, it was owned by Julius."[cxiv] Burns always looked at life on the bright side when he was taking a risk. When Burns signed the five-year contract, he jokingly said, "They (Caesar's Palace) wanted to make it a ten-year deal, but I didn't know if the hotel would last that long."[cxv] George Burns is a great example that shows you can leave a legacy when you take risks and live life on purpose.

Figure 5. George Burns[cxvi]

- Fredrick Douglass (African-American social reformer, orator, writer, and statesman)

Frederick Douglass was considered to be one of the principal leaders of the abolitionist movement, which fought to end slavery in the Unites States in the decades prior to the Civil War. Douglass participated in the American Anti-Slavery Society, and he became recognized as one of America's first great black speakers. Douglass won world fame when his autobiography was publicized in 1845; two years later he began publishing an antislavery paper called

the *North Star*. But before Douglass gained fame from his
autobiography and published paper, he had grown up as a
slave. He learned how to read and write from Sophia
Auld, wife of his slave master. After escaping from slavery, he became a leader of the abolitionist movement,
gaining note for his dazzling oratory and incisive anti-
slavery writing. Danish philosopher Søren Kierkegaard
declared, "No matter how deep an individual has sunk, he
can sink still deeper, and this 'can' is the object of anxiety." Douglass' anxiety was due to his experience escaping
the darkness of slavery. His feelings were characterized in
Frederick Douglass: A Biography by C. James Trotman, and
he was quoted:

> "May not this, after all, be God's work? May he
> not, for wise ends, have doomed me to this lot? A
> contest had been going on in my mind for years,
> between the clear consciousness of right and the
> plausible errors of superstition; between the wis-
> dom of manly courage, and the foolish weakness
> of timidity. The contest was now ended; the chain
> was severed; God and right stood vindicated. I
> was a FREEMAN, and the voice of peace and joy
> thrilled my heart."

Douglass served as an adviser to President Abraham
Lincoln during the Civil War and fought for the adoption
of constitutional amendments that guaranteed voting
rights and other civil liberties for blacks. Douglass pro-
vided a powerful voice for human rights during this period of American history and is still revered today for his
contributions against racial injustice.

Figure 6. Fredrick Douglass[cxvii]

These are excellent examples of people who had faith in their ability to succeed and refused to take no for an answer. The definition of success is "something that turns out as hoped for or has a favorable result." Failure is simply falling short of that favorable result but it is not the end. It is merely a speed bump on the highway of life. Or, as Henry Ford stated, "Failure is simply the opportunity to begin again, this time more intelligently."

Challenging B.S. (Belief System)

> *The habits of a vigorous mind are born in contending with difficulties.*
> —*Abigail Adams*

One of the most overused clichés in the business world is the term "thinking outside the box." Or maybe you've heard someone say, "We need a paradigm shift." Of course, you normally hear those comments or remarks

when someone is trying to get someone else to think differently about
something. In order to think differently about anything, you have to start by
challenging your own belief system. Naturally your belief system is characterized as a set of commonly supported and trusted ideas that people have
learned and that they live by. Consider these questions to examine your current belief system.

- Why do you believe what you believe?

- Why do you do what you do?

- What caused you to believe this in the first place? Where
  did you learn this? Is it valid?

- Can you think of a time when this belief would not have
  been held as true?

- In what way, if any, is this belief absurd or ridiculous?

- Has there ever been a time when this belief was not true
  or did not apply?

- Does this belief hold true in every situation? For everyone? Anywhere? Always?

- What are the exceptions to this belief?

These are just some of the questions, which can start you on the path to
challenging your belief system. But what these next questions can help you
really determine is how you see life.

- Do you see life as a test?

- Do you see life as a battle?

- Do you see life as something sacred?

If you see life as a test, then you're looking at it from a pass or fail state. If
you see life as a battle, then you're looking at it from a standpoint of always
looking for a fight. But if you see life as something sacred, then you're
wanting to take care of it. Based on those thoughts, this could be the
difference between keeping the status quo and truly challenging your belief

system. Wet concrete can be moved with ease and it is very impressionable before it dries or sets. But once it does set, it is in place for good unless a jack hammer is used to break it up. The same principle applies to our belief system. Our belief system must go through a process of change. Changing your beliefs starts by challenging your beliefs. Once you start to doubt what you believe, change starts to become possible.

Through my life experiences, I've learned that what I believe and think actually shapes everything that happens to me; but more importantly, it influences how I perceive and experience what occurs. If you stop to think about it, you can see this in action every single day. We all know people, who, despite the negative, horrible events that transpire in their lives or their relationships, are amazingly resilient. I love to see people who are able to turn the negativity, disappointment and failure around quickly and use it to fuel their continued growth and success. I believe that in order for that to happen, we have to be consistent in not placing blame when it comes to certain situations. For example, let's say you're trying to hammer a nail into a piece of wood and you mistakenly hit your thumb. If you're not careful you'll blame the hammer, the nail, or you'll blame whoever distracted you when you were trying to hammer the nail. The best thing to do is to question your hammering technique instead of all those other factors, which really had nothing to do with you hitting your thumb.

Have you ever thought about how you came to believe something when it didn't involve something someone else taught you? The process of forming a belief is as follows:

- You have an experience at one time in your life (whether it's good or bad).

- You have a thought about that experience (and you constantly think about it over and over).

- You then make a decision that it is based on a valid thought about that experience.

- You decided to believe it, and this forms a belief.

- You collect evidence in "the real world" to support your belief.

It all starts with how you view the experience, which leads to what kind of belief system you will have. And once you've formed a belief, you normally don't challenge it again unless you're forced to. This is because your belief feels true to you. And if it feels like it's true, it is true. I believe this is wrong because one person's truth could be a lie to someone else. As author Byron Katie told us in his book *Loving What Is: Four Questions That Can Change Your Life*, "A thought is harmless unless we believe it. It's not our thoughts, but our attachment to our thoughts, that causes suffering. Attaching to a thought means believing that it's true, without inquiring. A belief is a thought that we've been attaching to, often for years."[cxviii] Consequently, if you're not careful, you'll be holding on to a lie all because you failed to challenge your belief system that was based on the wrong information, which could lead to blame.

Whenever I'm in a situation and I try to place blame on someone or some event, I remind myself that blame is just an easy and contented way of looking for a scapegoat. Have you ever blamed someone for the speeding ticket you got? Did you blame your best friend because your classmate wouldn't go out with you? Did you blame someone for the test you failed? Did you blame someone because you gained weight? Those are just a few ways I've heard other people place blame. Naturalist and essayist John Burroughs maintained that, "You can get discouraged many times, but you are not a failure until you begin to blame somebody else and stop trying." Keep in mind that no one is walking around expecting to be a scapegoat willing to take the blame for the problems of the world. The term "scapegoat" was originated in the Old Testament book of Leviticus 16:20–22 when two goats were brought before the chief priest, who at the time was Aaron, to make atonement for the sins of Israel. Aaron drew lots between the two goats to determine which one of the goats would be sacrificed and which goat would be sent into the wilderness after he had symbolically laid the sins of the people upon the released goat.

"When Aaron has finished making atonement for the Most Holy Place, the tent of meeting and the altar, he shall bring forward the live goat. He is to lay both hands on the head of the live goat and confess over it all the wickedness and rebellion of the Israelites—all their sins—and put them on the goat's head. He shall send the goat away into the wilderness in the care of someone appointed for the task. The goat will carry on itself all their sins to a remote place; and the man shall release it in the wilderness." (NIV).

In modern terms, scapegoat is defined as a person who bears the sins of others, and it's often viewed with a negative undertone. So the next time you want to blame something on someone, just think about what the scapegoat represents in the Old Testament. The original scapegoat represented the sins of the nation, which God was comforting by forgetting their sins. Therefore, when we look to place blame, we are actually looking to put our flaws, imperfections, or faults on other people. And if you can accept this point, you're well on your way to challenging your belief system.

As I continue in the process of challenging my belief system, I apply the following strategies. First, I always try to be reasonable whenever my thoughts, beliefs, or ideas are challenged by specific situations or people. Is this an easy process? No! But I do believe that it starts by being on the lookout for specific reasonable and unreasonable behavior that you yourself might be projecting onto other people. I would advise you to look on the surface, and then look beneath the surface. Try to see the truth and get an understanding as to why something happened. Are you willing to listen to the views of others based on what they see? Are you willing to see that your perspective might be wrong? Whenever you ask yourself questions such as these, you're breaking through the shallow temperament of your belief system. A good strategy to becoming more reasonable is to challenge yourself to have the courage to admit that you're not perfect. It's good to admit that you make mistakes. Those who are self-righteous will never be able to challenge their belief system because they believe they're perfect and that they never make mistakes. People like this normally don't have a lot of friends. They normally are not open to change or to trying anything new. More importantly, they are usually not willing to put their beliefs aside to fully hear the views of those who might disagree with them. Reasonable people want to hear the other side of an argument. They want to learn something they didn't know prior to the discussion. Reasonable people want to change their thinking when they discover better thinking because they realize they don't have all the answers. And this is why it's important to challenge your belief system.

How would you rate yourself when it comes to being reasonable? If you're not satisfied with your answer, practice saying to yourself, "You know, I might be wrong." And then practice looking for those opportunities to make a change in your thinking. When you change your thinking, that's when you truly challenge your belief system.

Second, I try to always recognize when I'm being closed-minded. I view being closed-minded as being reluctant to change your mind or your thoughts even when you've been given a good reason to change your mind. Benjamin Franklin insisted, "Being ignorant is not so much a shame, as being unwilling to learn." Being closed-minded can be very obvious. Know that you're being closed-minded if you're unwilling to listen to the reasons of other people; if you're irritated by the reasons that people give you; and if you become defensive whenever you are involved in a discussion. These can be some very tough insights for you, which could challenge your belief system. Challenging a belief system is a constant work in progress because it's hard to know what you don't know. We're all so ingrained with things we were taught in our childhood that might be incorrect. It's not that our parents or guardians were trying to do us harm. Maybe they only taught the things they were taught or learned in passing. For those reasons alone, it's important to challenge your current belief system.

The third strategy I use in challenging my belief system is reprogramming my thinking process. You can reprogram your thinking by focusing and reframing. As I shared in the previous chapter, our energy flows to whatever we focus on. The best way to reprogram our thinking process is to focus on what we have and not the things we don't have. Author Robert Roots said, "It's not what you don't have, it's what you think you need that keeps you from being happy and successful." By focusing on what we have, we're reprogramming our thinking process by focusing on what's already possible. And when we focus on what's possible, we're more likely to be motivated to stay on the journey. Another way to reprogram our thinking process is through a method called reframing. Reframing involves focusing a person's attention on the same information previously available, but helping him or her view it differently so the implications can be recalibrated.[cxix]

Optical illusions are a good example of how reframing can challenge our belief system. See image 1.[cxx] If you notice in the picture below, if viewed by blinking both eyes, you can see the face from the front view and from the side view. Which face did you see first, the side or the front? If you only see one view, why? As you can see, both options are made available only through the reframing method, which would otherwise not be feasible or acceptable. Reframing is just picturing the possibilities of what the object is actually showing. To look at this photo one way, you might have to look at it with one eye open; but if you open both eyes and blink, you can possibly see the other image that might be harder for you to see. The same in life is true as opportunities to think new and different ways may be all around us, but we fail to see them because we don't challenge our thinking. Reframing is another way of stepping outside of our trained patterns of perceptions to see the possibilities.

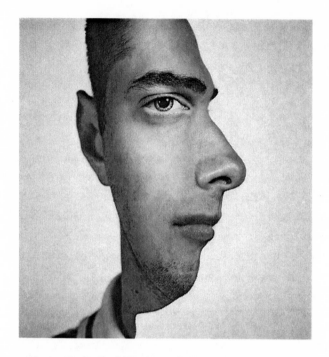

Figure 7. Optical illusions challenge our beliefs.[cxxi]

As I mentioned earlier in this chapter, Muhammad Ali was a great thinker in motivating and encouraging himself to become the world champion. Ali also showed a great example of how to reframe your thoughts when he was put in jail for refusing to go into the military. Ali claimed that his belief as a practicing Muslim prohibited him from fighting in Vietnam. Ali was immediately stripped of his title by the New York State Athletic Commission (NYSAC) and the World Boxing Association (WBA) and effectively banned from boxing for three-and-a-half years.[cxxii] After all the hard work and effort to become champion, you would think that he would have been upset and angry. Ali reframed this situation to see that this was an opportunity to find his soul in his race and his religious beliefs. Ali is proof that sometimes having something taken away from you can be all the sweeter when you have the opportunity to take it back. His phenomenal comeback as a champion and his boxing legacy is great proof of what's possible when you reframe anything that happens to you.

As you continue to look at what's happening in your life, I hope it tells a more positive, powerful story. It's not about lying to yourself or hiding your head in the sand. Instead, it's about telling a story about what's happened so that it will allow for the highest degree of hope, encouragement and inspiration possible. As you challenge your belief system, know and imagine what's possible when you think outside the box, or even when you create circles, triangles, and squares. As you challenge your beliefs, know that your change in mind will become possible. And as that change in mind becomes possible, then and only then will you be able to live life on purpose.

Chapter 5
Live your purpose!

If you think the work you do is of little meaning or little importance, consider the following: Little drops of water and little grains of sand lead to the mighty oceans and most beautiful beaches.

—Dr. Samuel Jones

NOW THAT YOU'VE discovered your purpose and defined your purpose, it is time to live your purpose. One of my favorite explanations of how to live life on purpose is the comparison of freedom and self-discipline given by Apostle Paul in his letter to the Corinthian church in 1 Corinthians 9:22–23. He wrote, "To the weak I became weak, to win the weak. I have become all things to all people so that by all possible means I might save some. I do all this for the sake of the gospel that I may share in its blessings. Do you not know that in a race all the runners run, but only one gets the prize? Run in such a way as to get the prize."[cxxiii] (NIV) Paul was encouraging believers to be persistent about doing what they have been called to do. The Greek Philosopher, Aristotle, also shared with us how we can be persistent in our doing when he said, "Whatever we learn to do, we learn by actually doing it; men come to be builders, for instance, by building, and harp players by playing the harp. In the same way, by doing just acts we come to be just; by doing self-controlled acts, we come to be self-controlled; and by doing brave acts, we become brave." Both of these commands to be persistent in our actions encourage us to actively live our purpose.

However, I don't want you to get to the end of this book only to say, "Now that I've discovered and I've defined my purpose, I'm going to start living it someday." It's easy to keep planning to do things tomorrow. For example, have you ever made any of the following promises to yourself? "I'll do it when I finish with college," or "I'll do it when we get our credit card paid off," or "I'll do it when the kids are grown and out of the house," or "I'll do it when I stop drinking or when I quit smoking." The point is that it's easy to say, "I'll do it someday." Just keep this in mind, whenever you say you'll do "something when ..." what you're really saying is that you're not ready to make the commitment to get whatever that thing is done. I've learned to never take any day or person for granted. Hence, I don't ever delay my tasks, my goals, my dreams, or even my life's purpose until "Someday." Author Denis Waitley refers to "Someday" as "Someday Isle," which sounds like "Someday I'll." He describes it as an imaginary island in the sea where people like to go to get lost away from their responsibilities. It's a place without the distractions of having to do what you know needs to be done. "Someday I'll do this," and "Someday I'll do that." I've learned that when it comes to living my purpose, I must avoid this island at all costs because being or living on this island only keeps me from my destination of living my purpose.

Now that you're motivated to get started, I want to share with you three mechanisms for living your purpose. **I call these the three Ps of living your purpose: passion, practice, and proof.** If you can envision a three-legged stool, the stool would be supported by all of the legs. If one is weaker or shorter than the others, the whole thing will topple. All three legs are needed to support the stool in the same way you need all three mechanisms to work together to support your purpose in order for you to live your purpose. (See Figure 8.)

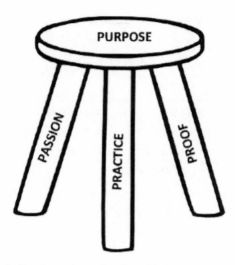

Figure 8. Dr. Jones' mechanism for living your purpose.

Passion

> *Passion. It lies in all of us. Sleeping ... waiting ... and though unwanted, un-*
> *bidden, it will stir ... open its jaws and howl. It speaks to us ... guides us.*
> *Passion rules us all. And we obey. What other choice do we have? Passion is the*
> *source of our finest moments. The joy of love ... the clarity of hatred ... the*
> *ecstasy of grief. It hurts sometimes more than we can bear. If we could live without*
> *passion, maybe we'd know some kind of peace. But we would be hollow. Empty*
> *rooms, shuttered and dank. Without passion, we'd be truly dead.*
> *—Joss Whedon*

Can you recognize passion in action? Probably, but you must be looking for it. As I was thinking about the subject of "passion" while writing this book, there were many examples that came to mind. I'll share four examples, which have really inspired me to let my passion flow. Can you think of a time when you were passionate about doing something? Or maybe you were passionate about sharing your opinion? Did you think about what other people thought about you? Did you think about how your voice sounded?

Did you even think about what the consequences might be? Since I've learned what my purpose in life is, I don't even consider these kinds of questions as I continue to live my purpose. And I must attest that once you're in your purpose and you allow your passion to flow through, you won't even be bothered by what other people think or how your voice sounds. When you're doing and living your passion, you couldn't care less about those things that are not important. Swiss philosopher, poet, and critic Henri Frederic Ameil reminded us, "Without passion, man is a mere latent force and a possibility, like the flint which awaits the shock of the iron before it can give forth its spark." Your passion is really the foundation for your desire to live your purpose. In the great pursuit of living my purpose with passion, I try to answer these questions: Who am I living my purpose for? What examples can I look at that show me passion in action? And my last question: Can others view my passion in action as I live my purpose?

Accordingly, who would you be living your purpose for? It's good to do things for your family. It's good to do things for perfect strangers. And it's good to give back to your community. As Apostle Paul reminded us in the book of Colossians, "Whatever you do, work at it with all your heart, as working for the Lord, not for human masters, since you know that you will receive an inheritance from the Lord as a reward. It is the Lord Christ you are serving." (NIV)[cxxiv] Paul wrote the book of Colossians while in prison as he was trying to send encouraging words to believers in Colosse. As you read his writings, you can tell that Paul never lost his passion for rescuing the church by reminding them of who God is and making God known to the nonbelievers. The main reason why I choose to share the story of Paul is because I admire the passion he expressed in his writings, and also because I can relate to his journey. Acts 9:4 tells the story of how Paul changed his life. Paul's original name was Saul before his encounter with the spirit of Jesus Christ on the road to Damascus. Saul was traveling on that road to persecute all the believers and followers of Jesus Christ. Saul was challenged on this journey as he was struck down by a blinding light, brighter than the noonday sun. Saul heard a voice say to him, "Saul, Saul, why do you persecute me?" (NIV) The blinding light was the risen Christ as he questioned Saul about persecuting the followers of Christ. The men traveling with Saul only heard the sound, but they didn't see the blinding light. Saul was blinded, and he was led by the hand into Damascus to the house of Judas on Straight Street. Saul did not eat or drink anything and remained blind for three days. And this is the experience that changed Saul's passion from persecuting believers to passionately speaking and writing to non-believers to convert them. When he began converting non-believers, Saul began using the name Paul.

I can relate to Saul/Paul's experience in several ways. One of the ways I can relate is that I wasn't always a believer in Jesus Christ. Like Saul, I always questioned why believers would want to persuade others to believe in God or believe in Jesus just because I didn't. And like Saul, I was blind to the fact that I was a sinner and that I needed a savior to save me from my sins. And like Saul, I was blinded by the fact that the risen Christ spoke to me to inform me that I couldn't save myself. I was a self-interested, self-centered person who only thought about myself. I thought I was always right and that everybody else was wrong. But once I began to grow up and listen to the wisdom of my grandmother, I came to realize that I was acting like Saul when he was a non-believer. Instead of persecuting others, I was persecuting myself because I was the only person who was being hurt in the process. And like Saul, I realized I had to get on the "Straight Street," and this is what changed my life. Getting on the Straight Street for me meant doing several things. First, I confessed that I was a sinner. Next, I confessed that Jesus Christ is Lord, and I believed in my heart that he died for my sins and that he rose on the third day. Once I accepted that as the undeniable, irrefutable, unapologetic truth, this is also when I realized that he rose in me. And like Saul, once I was humbled, my life began to change. Even though I didn't change my name, I did change what my name represented. Now that I've become a minister of the word of God, I can envision myself similar to the Prophet Samuel in the Old Testament who was doing the work of the Lord. And like Paul and Samuel, I want my passion to show through everything that I do. As you continue on your journey, be sure that you have the passion to keep your three-legged purpose standing tall. As author Joseph Campbell says, "Passion will move men beyond themselves, beyond their shortcomings, and even beyond their failures." Benjamin Franklin insisted that if passion drives you, let your reason hold the reins. And in the words of Paul in Romans 12:5–8, his letter to the Roman church, "So in Christ we, though many, form one body, and each member belongs to all the others. We have different gifts, according to the grace given to each of us. If your gift is prophesying, then prophesy in accordance with your faith; if it is serving, then serve; if it is teaching, then teach; if it is to encourage, then give encouragement; if it is giving, then give generously; if it is to lead, do it diligently; if it is to show mercy, do it cheerfully."[cxxv] (NIV)

The next example of someone living out his life's purpose with passion is author, television actor, and radio and television talk show host Steve Harvey. Harvey was the youngest of five children born to Eloise and Jesse Harvey in West Virginia, where his father was a coal miner who passed away from black lung disease.[cxxvi] The passion that Harvey had to become a television personality was tested at an early age. At the age of nine, an elementary school teacher and his classmates doubted his goal of one day starring on television. He was asked in class what he wanted to be when he grew up. And instead of any of the usual responses like teacher, firefighter, doctor, or lawyer, he said that he wanted to be on television. His classmates laughed at him, and his teacher thought he was being the class clown. Harvey later pointed out, "I wanted to be on television since I was nine years old, but I didn't make it until I was thirty-eight."[cxxvii]

After finishing college at West Virginia University, Harvey spent his early twenties working at a number of jobs—insurance salesman, postman, even wannabe professional boxer—without finding anything that really seemed like his true calling. He eventually found that calling on the stage, performing standup comedy for the first time in 1985. After honing his act through several years of performances in small clubs, he made it to the final round of the Second Annual Johnnie Walker National Comedy Search in 1989.[cxxviii] And this is when his career began to take off, but he always showed passion in everything he did, from the MC of the *Kings of Comedy* tour to *The Steve Harvey Morning Show* on the radio to *The Steve Harvey* sitcom on the WB channel, even to several books he has authored. Harvey maintained, "I've been an everyday person for thirty-eight years. I'm now fifty-three and I'm thinking about the responsibility of being a father, and my listeners and I've just gotten to a place where it's got to be more than jokes. I know it sounds corny, but I'm starting really to think about my life in terms of 'What are they going to say about me?' Do I want it just to be said, 'This guy was a king of comedy?' Well, it's not enough. Been there, done that. The sense of wanting to do something meaningful is upon me now."[cxxix]

Harvey's example is proof that his passion is flowing through his life. I like the fact that he is making a difference in everything he touches. Harvey and his wife founded The Steve and Marjorie Harvey Foundation with the mission of providing outreach to fatherless children and young adults by promoting educational enrichment, one-on-one mentoring, and global service initiatives that will cultivate the next generation of responsible leaders.[cxxx] And based on my life story and the absence of my father, I would love to work with The Steve and Marjorie Harvey Foundation because I see the passion in it. So, if you know Steve Harvey, please let him know that I'm interested in working with him on a project.

Another inspiring story of passion that really caught my attention is that of real-estate entrepreneur, author, and political activist Donahue Peebles. Raised by his single, teenage mother, a young Peebles vowed that he would gain financial security for himself—a promise that drove him to take an unconventional path to success. Peebles built the largest African-American-owned real estate development firm by mastering the art of risk taking. And as you read more about his story, you'll see and sense his passion as he crossed many roadblocks and challenges as a young black man in America pursuing his dreams and his purpose.

Peebles grew up in Washington, D.C., after his parents divorced. When he told the story of how he became interested in real estate, Peebles said, "I was inducted into the real estate business as a child. My mother was a secretary, but she went to night school to get her brokerage license and worked as a sales agent. Later, she opened her own real estate brokerage firm. During the summer of my senior year of high school, I worked with her appraising homes, learning the business. I also worked on Capitol Hill as a page and as an intern for two congressmen, Rep. John Conyers of Michigan and Rep. Ron Dellums of California. I had a pretty grueling schedule, but I got to see how politics and business interacted."[cxxxi] In 1979, Peebles started his real estate career as an appraiser, and within three years, he opened his own firm and had clients such as the United States Department of Housing and Urban Development and major financial and banking institutions. In 1983, at the age of 23, Peebles' career took a meteoric rise after Mayor Marion Barry appointed him to the District of Columbia's Board of Equalization and Review (now known as the Board of Real Property Assessment and Appeal). In 1984, he became chairman of the board, the youngest chairman of any board in Washington, D.C., history. He served as chairman until 1988.[cxxxii]

I believe his passion to become successful flowed through the risks he took. As told by a writer at *Inc.* magazine, Peebles was a powerful player in real estate development in Washington, D.C., in the early 1990s, but was hardly a national figure. Then, on a family vacation in Miami, he decided to bid on the redevelopment of the grand but tired Royal Palms, a 417-room resort at the end of South Beach's wealthy Ocean Drive. This project took six years to complete, and the resort was renamed the Royal Palm Crowne Plaza, the first African-American-owned resort.[cxxxiii] In 2003, it was the second largest hotel on South Beach, and it brought in more than 16 million dollars in revenue.[cxxxiv] And this was the project that solidified Peebles' reputation as an aggressive and passionate businessman.

In May 2009, *Forbes* listed Peebles in the top ten of the wealthiest black Americans, and *Fortune* magazine had estimated his net worth at $350 million.[cxxxv] But when you really get to the gist of his story, you realize that his story is not just about wealth, but you can sense his passion in giving back and making the world a better place by providing opportunities. Peebles maintained, "I take being a minority businessperson as a responsibility. My grandfather was a doorman for forty years at a Marriott in D.C. And I'm going to give opportunities to minorities and women, both of whom are underrepresented in my industry. But all too frequently people come up with excuses as to why they can't succeed. They say it's too difficult. They can't get a job. They end up giving up their goals before they have a chance to fulfill them. I could have made a lot of excuses in my career, but the No. 1 ingredient to success is to not accept failure."cxxxvi I'm thankful for the example of passion that Peebles has displayed with his life because he is proof of what you can do when you allow your passion to drive you. So follow Peebles' example, and continue to take risks by allowing your passion to be your driving force to follow your purpose.

And the last example of passion that I want to share with you is that of Harry Johnson. Johnson is an entrepreneur and lawyer from St. Louis, Missouri. Johnson has been the President and CEO of the Washington, D.C., Martin Luther King, Jr. National Memorial Project Foundation, Inc. since 2002.cxxxvii The reason Harry Johnson's story is important is because of the many times he had doubts about the fundraising efforts to build the $120 million King Memorial on the Mall in Washington, D.C., yet he never gave up. Alpha Phi Alpha Fraternity historian Robert Harris, a professor of history at Cornell University in Ithaca, New York, said the idea for the monument started twenty-eight years earlier when George Sealey and his wife, sitting at their kitchen table, said there should be a tribute to King in Washington. Harris said they got the idea after watching President Reagan sign into law the King Holiday Bill in the fall of 1983.cxxxviii Sealey brought together four other fraternity brothers and from there the idea became a national mission of the Alpha Phi Alpha Fraternity. After years of producing fiscal and fundraising plans, drawings and blueprints, and galvanizing public support, Alpha Phi Alpha, Inc. persuaded Congress and key elements of the executive branch, including the Department of the Interior and the White House, to green light the project.cxxxix The House of Representatives passed Joint Resolution 70 authorizing Alpha Phi Alpha Fraternity, Inc. to establish a memorial in Washington, D.C., to honor Dr. Martin Luther King, Jr. on September 28, 1996. The Senate followed soon after, and on July 16, 1998, President Clinton signed a Joint Congressional Resolution authorizing the building of a memorial.cxl

Johnson explained in an article in the *Huffington Post* series called "The Inspirationals" how he dealt with some dark days when he didn't think they would be able to raise the funds for the project. But he also shared how he had inspirational days, which helped him understand and know that they would raise the funds needed for the project. Johnson explained that his basic pitch was that contributing to the project would mean something different for everyone.

> "If someone came and said, 'We don't do brick and mortar,' I would tell them the old rule I learned in law school. The first rule you learn in law school is that there are rules of law. The second rule you learn in law school is there is an exception to every rule. So I would simply say this is the exception. If someone had personal doubts, I would say, who should really pay for the memorial of Dr. King? Should it be corporations? Foundations? Should it be high-dollar net-worth individuals? Or people like you and I? And I think you answer that by saying, anyone who would ever benefit from anything Dr. King said or did should pay. And when you sit back and take a deep breath, that's all of us."[cxli]

Johnson's passion flowed through the fundraising process because he always believed in himself and in what he was doing. Johnson said that his mother taught him very early that he could be whoever he wanted to be, that he could do whatever he wanted to do, and all he had to do was to believe in himself. You can sense Johnson's passion as he expressed his joy and pride in the challenge. He insisted, "I believe I'm just as good as the president of the United States, I just happen to not be the president. But I can walk, talk, and be just as proud as I am of myself as he is of himself, or any world leader. And I think that's part of the leadership skills that we learn, you need to lead: You need to know who you are. And then you need to lead for a cause—and what better cause could there be than this? So I took it and ran with it."[cxlii]

And not only did Johnson run with the King Memorial fundraising efforts, but he shared those efforts with the world when the King monument was dedicated on August 28, 2011, on the forty-eighth anniversary of the March on Washington and the *I Have a Dream* speech. Through the hard work and passion of Johnson and many others, visitors to the King Memorial are now able to enjoy the fruits of their labor by keeping the spirit and history of the work of Dr. King alive. I would encourage you to visit this memorial because it will definitely have an impact on your life. Below is just a partial list of individuals and businesses who contributed considerable sums towards the completion of the Martin Luther King, Jr. Memorial.[cxliii]

General Motors: $10 million

Tommy Hilfiger: $6 million

Alpha Phi Alpha Fraternity: $3.5 million

NBA: $3 million

Bill and Melinda Gates: $3 million

Walt Disney Co.: $2.7 million

Toyota: $2.5 million

Verizon: $2 million

Delta Airlines: $1.5 million

General Electric: $1.2 million

FedEx: $1 million

Sheila Johnson, BET co-founder: $1 million

NFL Players Association: $1 million

George Lucas, *Star Wars* creator: $1 million

Viacom/BET/MTV: $1 million

Wal-Mart: $1 million

Morehouse College: $500,000

CBS: $500,000

Procter & Gamble: $431,200

American Federation of Teachers: $300,000

Lehman Brothers: $250,000

Alpha Kappa Alpha Sorority: $170,000

Delta Sigma Theta Sorority: $137,000

General Mills: $100,000

The Embassy of South Africa: $100,000

So, do you think you can find the passion to do something that is life changing? Did the work of the Apostle Paul impact you? How about the work of Steve Harvey? What about the work of Donahue Peebles? Or better yet, what about the work of Harry Johnson? The point is that there are so many examples of people living and working with passion that we don't have an excuse when it comes to having passion in our own purpose. So as you continue on your journey, remember that your purpose is the reason for your journey and your passion is the fire that lights your way. So continue your journey and continue to let your light shine so that you'll know the way.

Practice

The way anything is developed is through practice, practice, practice, practice,
practice, practice, practice, practice, practice, and more practice.

—*Joyce Meyer*

No matter what you want to accomplish in life, you must start with practice. Legendary college football coach Paul "Bear" Bryant was quoted saying, "It's not the will to win that matters … everyone has that. It's the will to prepare to win that matters." I can admit that I didn't always have the will to prepare to win, whether that was in athletics or in life. I can remember vividly playing basketball in high school, and head coach Willie Earl Thomas always challenged us. We normally had a scrimmage at the end of every practice, with the starters versus the second string team. I was always a starter, and we would scrimmage for about twenty minutes. Thomas often stopped the scrimmage with about five minutes left. The starters were usually ahead by fifteen to twenty points against the second teamers. But what Coach Thomas would do next made me upset at the time, until I quite understood what he was trying to teach us. He would give the second teamers the starters' points and the starters would take the second teamers' score.

Coach Thomas did this to see what kind of fight the starters would have if they were down fifteen to twenty points with five minutes left in a game. The lesson I got from this is that it's easy to be good and play well when you're up by twenty points. The challenge is to see how you practice and play when you're down. I'm thankful to Coach Thomas for teaching that point to us then because it helps me today to remember to always practice everything that I want to do well. It helps me to practice with consistency, no matter what the focus of the activity is. I've learned that practice doesn't always make you perfect, but it does make for improvement.

Did you know that practice is really a way for you to demonstrate the gifts and talents that you already have? I know of many examples of people who overinflate their abilities and downplay the importance of practice. They don't see the importance in it. One of my favorite examples is when former NBA All-Star basketball player Allen Iverson went on a tirade with reporters as he was being interviewed about missing a day of practice when he played for the Philadelphia 76ers. This is the transcript of the Iverson interview with sports reporters.

> "If a coach says I missed practice, and y'all hear it, then that's that. I might've missed one practice this year. But if somebody says, he doesn't come to practice—it can be one practice, out of all the practices this year—then that's enough ... But it's easy to talk about, it's easy to sum it up when you just talk about practice. We sittin' in here, I'm supposed to be the franchise player, and we in here talkin' about practice. I mean listen, we talkin' 'bout practice. Not a game ... not the game that I go out there and die for, and play every game like it's my last. Not the *game*. We talkin' 'bout *practice*, man. I mean how silly is that? We talkin' 'bout practice. I know I'm supposed to be there, I know I'm supposed to lead by example. I know that, and I'm not shovin' it aside, you know, like it don't mean anything. I know it's important, I do. I honestly do. But we talkin' 'bout practice, man. What are we talkin' about? Practice? We talkin' about practice, man. [Reporters laughing] We ain't talkin' 'bout the game, we talkin' 'bout practice, man. When you come into the arena, and you see me play,

you see me play, don't you? You see me give everything I got, right? But we talkin' 'bout practice right now. [Reporter: 'But it's an issue that your coach raised.'] We talkin' 'bout practice. Man look, I hear you, it's funny to me too. I mean, it's strange to me too. But we talkin' 'bout practice, man. We not even talkin' 'bout the game, the actual game, when it matters. We talkin' 'bout practice."[cxliv]

Thus, according to Iverson during that particular interview, the art of practice is really not that important. And don't get me wrong, I'm a former basketball player so I understand what Iverson is saying; but I don't agree with what he was saying. In my opinion, what he was really saying is that since he gave his heart and soul to the game every time he stepped on the floor, he felt that he should have some leeway to do what he wanted when it came to practice. I could tell that when he said, 'I'm supposed to be the franchise player ... I know I'm supposed to be there ... I know I'm supposed to lead by example.' When I heard those comments, it was obvious to me that he wanted special rules, which only applied to him. But you show your true greatness when you know you're gifted and talented and you still take practice seriously.

In the book *Talent is Overrated: What Really Separates World Class Performers from Everybody Else*, author Geoff Colvin highlights studies that show greatness can be developed by anyone, in any field through the process he calls "deliberate practice." Colvin suggested deliberate practice is characterized by several elements. He insisted that the activity is designed specifically to improve performance (often with the help of a coach or teacher); the process can be repeated a lot; feedback on the results is continuously available; the activity is highly demanding mentally, and the process isn't much fun.[cxlv] Let's consider each of those characteristics of deliberate practice and what it implies.

Deliberate Practice is Designed to Improve Performance

Many people practice by mindlessly repeating an activity over and over without any clear goal of what they want to accomplish. For example, let's say that a basketball player wants to improve personal stats such as his free throw shooting percentage. The average player will go to the gym and shoot a certain amount of free throws without thinking much about specific ways to improve. And, of course, five hundred free throws later, the player most likely still hasn't improved the free throw shot at all. In fact, the free throw shooting percentage may have gotten worse if the player didn't gain confidence in the ability to make them.

On the other hand, a great basketball player will get help. The player will use deliberate practice designed with clear objectives and goals and often with a coach or teacher. When this top performer practices, the player and coach will usually break down the skill into sharply defined elements. They will then work intently on the element that needs the most improvement. And during the entire practice session, they focus solely on that one aspect. For instance, the basketball player may use a free throw practice session to solely focus on foot placement when making a free throw. Most people don't realize that their foot stance is one of the most important aspects of a free throw shot. That's why it's important to having a coach or a teacher to help you with your practice. Coaches have the knowledge and experience to break down your skill into specific elements to help you in your needed areas. They can also see you in ways that you can't see yourself, and then help you focus on the items that you need to work on the most.

There's a reason the best golfer in the world continues to have coaches and mentors throughout his career. According to the Official World Gold ranking, Tiger Woods has been the number one golf player in the world for a total of 674 weeks.[cxlvi] Woods understood the power of an outside eye and the opinion of his father when he first started playing golf at two years old. Wood's father, Earl, was a teacher and he had a lifelong passion for sports. Earl Woods wrote in his book *Training a Tiger*, "I love to teach. I was already properly trained to play golf and I took over new ground in training Tiger at an unthinkable age."[cxlvii] Tiger received his first metal club, a putter from his dad, at the age of seven months old. Tiger began watching his dad swing the club, when he was several months old sitting in his high chair in the garage. He would watch his dad hit golf balls into a net for hours on end. Earl wrote, "For Tiger, this was like watching a movie being run over and over and over from his view."[cxlviii] And, as of today, Tiger has repeatedly credited his father for his success in golf. Earl had Tiger training at an early age designed for success. He chose specific elements for performance for Tiger to focus on at each stage of his learning process. American management consultant, author, and educator Noel M. Tichy illustrates the point by drawing three concentric circles. The inner circle labeled "comfort zone," the middle circle labeled "learning zone," and the outer circle labeled "panic zone."[cxlix] He insisted that your learning zone is just outside of your comfort zone. It is really hard to learn anything when you're comfortable. You must stretch yourself by taking risks to do the unordinary. But if you stretch yourself too much, you'll end up in the panic zone. In the panic zone, learning is not taking place at all. (See Figure 9)[cl]

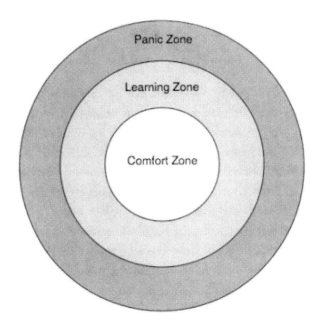

Figure 9. Tichy's Performance Zone

The Practice Activity Can be Regularly Repeated

Any great athlete will tell you that repetition is probably one of the most important aspects of any skill set. If you want to be good any anything, you'll have to put in the time and effort to constantly repeat it. The most important difference between deliberate practice and performing the task when it counts is high repetition. But know that doing something repeatedly, especially if it is wrong, will not make way for success when it's time to do it right. This is why it's important to have a coach or a teacher to assist you in order to have the fundamental techniques in your deliberate practice. As author and motivational speaker Norman Vincent Peale insisted, repetition of the same thought or physical action develops into a habit, which repeated frequently enough, becomes an automatic reflex. So practice does not become perfect but it does makes for improvement.

The Practice Activity Provides Feedback on a Continual Basis

Getting feedback on practice activities can be easy only if the individual practicing has a humble enough mindset in order to accept the feedback and make the proper changes needed in order to become the best. Some people struggle because they don't understand the difference between feedback and criticism. Some take feedback to be criticism, but they don't understand the difference between the two. I believe criticism is driven by frustration and fears of the giver, and the recipient begins to take that personally. This message then turns the recipient against the giver and the giver tends to express that he is the only one who knows how to fix the recipient's problem. On the other hand, feedback is driven by respect, concern, and support. Feedback is an honest approach with the desire to have positive intentions from both the giver and the recipient. Both want to do what's right for the relationship. Feedback supports the ideal that the *relationship of the giver and the recipient is a partnership* in order to make the recipient better at the skill that is being practiced.

The Practice Activity is Highly Demanding Mentally

There are examples of many different disciplines throughout Colvin's book ranging from surgeons to taxi drivers to chess players to sportsmen to public speakers to musicians to computer programmers and politicians and beyond. Based on Colvin's observation, the only limits that we all bring when it comes to deliberate practice are the limitations in our mind. In order to get your desired results, you must have mental toughness and resilience because your activities, whether physical or mental, will require both. At the root of all mental training in your desired area of expertise is this question: Are you mentally tough enough to bring out the best in yourself?

The Practice Activity isn't Much Fun

Learning to improve a skill to a higher level is tremendously hard work. There are no magic buttons that will bypass practice. Doing things we know how to do well is pleasurable, but this is exactly the opposite of what deliberate practice expects of us. At that point, you'd be trying to seek out those things that you're not good at to get better at them. And as you constantly practice on this skill set, pain will be identified, which can emphasize the activities that will make you better. As the saying goes, 'no pain, no gain.' And as you repeat this practice process, you would be forcing yourself to see what isn't right so that you can keep building your skills. The good news is that this will make you stand out if you have any competition.

The scripture tells me that to whom much is given, much is required. So if you have been given much when it comes to your skills, your talents, etc., then you should expect much more to be required from you. Practice isn't the thing you do to become good; it's that thing you do over and over to become great. I truly believe that if Iverson had to do it all over again, he would probably do things a little differently when it came to his view about practice. Consequently, how does one think about practice? Do you like to practice the things you want to be good at? Or do you complain when it comes to practice? These are some great questions tone should consider when it comes to practicing the things you need to do in order to live your purpose. If you answer these questions with answers such as: "I don't like practice," or "I usually complain when it comes to practicing any skill that will help me fulfill and live my purpose," then you might not be doing the things that will ultimately lead you to your purpose. In order to practice the things you need to, you must keep in mind your personal intelligence style, which was mentioned in an earlier chapter.

Proof

The best way to show that a stick is crooked is not to argue about it or to spend time denouncing it, but to lay a straight stick alongside it.
—D.L. Moody

Universal Studios theme park in Orlando, Florida, is one of my favorite theme parks to visit. There are games and rides for people of all ages. One of my favorite things to do is to ride the roller coasters. I don't really consider myself a thrill seeker, but I do enjoy the adrenalin rush from a good, steep rollercoaster. I also like to see the adults who wimp out when they are challenged by teenagers to do those death-defying rides. Once the adults have been challenged and they back down, the adults often claim they're not afraid to ride the coaster. And every time I've heard an adult say that, I think to myself, "The proof is in the pudding." Have you ever had a similar situation when you made that statement? I find myself thinking that when I hear people say they can do something, but they refuse to do it. "The proof is in the pudding" is a shortened version of the very old proverb, "The proof of the pudding is in the eating," and it meant that you had to try the pudding to know whether it was good or not. So what does this have to do with your purpose? This means that the only way you'll see the proof of living your purpose is to just do it and then to examine your results. Like pudding, you must taste your purpose in order to know the proof of what you have.

Another instance about confirming the proof you have would be the saying, "Show me the money." Show me the money is a phrase commonly used by people wanting proof that something is true. But in this case, I want to use it to show proof of purpose. "Show me the money" is a memorable saying from one of my favorite movies of all-time, *Jerry Maguire*. In this movie, a successful sports agent, Jerry Maguire, had an epiphany. Maguire questioned his purpose in life and he put all his thoughts into a mission statement. Armed with his new outlook on life and how he would do business differently, he was immediately met with indifference from his superiors. As a result, he was fired for expressing his new philosophy on doing business purposefully. He then decided to put his new way of business to the test as an independent sports agent, and the only athlete who stayed with him was Rod Tidwell. In one of my favorite scenes in the movie, Maguire was on the phone with Tidwell begging to remain Tidwell's agent. Tidwell told Maguire that he would keep him on as his agent, but then said, "That's what I'm gonna do for you, but this is what you're gonna do for me." Tidwell then insisted Maguire repeat after him, "Show me the money." Maguire's first several attempts to please his client were half-hearted and feeble, but Tidwell continued to cheer his agent on until Maguire was screaming into the phone, "Show me the money." Once Maguire convinced Tidwell with his excitement, he hung up the phone with thoughts of uncertainty.[cli]

Now is the time for you to "show me your purpose." Now that you're on the path to show proof of your purpose, do you have everything you need? Do you need to add any other ingredients to the pursuit of your purpose, perhaps perseverance? Do you need to add knowledge and expertise in some area to show proof of your purpose? Or do you need to add a mentor to your purpose process? You will be able to answer questions like these only after you have some proof about what your true purpose is in life. You must be sure that you know who you are. There's an old saying that inside every individual, there are six people who live there. And these six people tend to show up based on the given situation. The six people are who you are reputed to be, who you are expected to be, who you were in the past, who you wish to be, who you think you are, and who you really are.

Author Terry Pearce said, "There are many people who think they want to be matadors, only to find themselves in the ring with two thousand pounds of bull bearing down on them and to then discover that what they really wanted was to wear tight pants and hear the crowd roar." Can you relate to this story? Is there an area in your life where you just want to get the praise or the trophy without doing the heavy lifting or the hard work? Well, when it comes to having proof that you're living your purpose, you must have passion and be consistent in your practice. Therefore, if you decide to jump into the ring with that two thousand pound bull, it will be because of your love of the experience, the escapade, and the love of accomplishing something. And that's the same when it comes to you jumping into that ring with your purpose. It will be because you see your purpose as something that you love and the possibility of creating something new. Also, you'll be on a journey towards becoming a better person and having the opportunity to accomplish something that maybe you didn't think was possible. I'm constantly telling myself when I'm pursing my goals, dreams, and aspirations: It's not what you pursue, but it's who you become in the process. So when you know your 'proof is in the pudding,' or you're able to 'show me the money,' then you will be able to get to work preparing to produce as much proof as possible.

Three cornerstones of proof have definitely made an impact on my life and how I live my life on purpose. **The cornerstones of proof are examples, strategy, and feedback**. As I discuss each cornerstone in detail, examine your life and see how they can become a foundation for everything you do as it relates to your purpose.

Examples

The first cornerstone in the proof of living your purpose is an example. We all need examples of how to do something well. These examples can also serve as extra motivation. Arguably the greatest basketball player of all-time, Michael Jordan, always insisted that Julius "Dr. J" Erving was the one who set the example for him on the basketball court. Jordan modeled his attitude after Dr. J. During Erving's Hall of Fame induction speech, he maintained that every day since he was seven years old, he had demanded more from himself than anyone else could possibly expect. Michael Jordan used the example that Dr. J had lain before him and applied it to his life. Michael

Jordan insisted that, "No one has a higher demand on myself than me. I never competed with other people. I competed with what my best could possibly be. Competing with other people will only push you so hard and so far." Now I think about the talents and efforts of both Hall of Famers when either of their names is mentioned.

Jordan and Erving are great examples who illustrate how to achieve a desirable result. There are so many other examples of the proof that people are living their purpose; it's easy to look around and find several. For another example of perseverance, consider seventy-four year old law student Benjamin Roll. Roll had already become a success in life, but there was one thing he wanted to do, and that was to pass the California bar exam in order to become a lawyer. Roll had already served in World War II, he had previously worked in the Appalachian oil fields, and he was the father of eight children. And it was on the fourteenth try that Roll was able to pass the essay part of the bar exam. At the age of seventy-four, after six years and fourteen tests, he finally passed. Roll said humbly, "It was hard, but actually I felt very comfortable that I had passed … I'm not used to failure."[clii]

Consider another example of commitment by the Delaney sisters. Sarah "Sadie" L. Delany and Elizabeth "Bessie" Delany were the daughters of a former slave who became the first African-American elected bishop in the Episcopal Church in the United States. The sisters were civil rights pioneers, and when they were interviewed for a feature story, their story turned into a book.[cliii] The book was titled *Having Our Say: The Delany Sister's First 100 years.* Yes, that is correct, with the help of others, these sisters were able to write their first book at 100 years old, which was on the *New York Times* best-seller list for 105 weeks,[cliv] and has sold more than five million copies, according to author and former *New York Times* reporter Amy Hill Hearth, who interviewed the sisters for the book. The book went on to inspire a Broadway play in 1995 and a CBS television film in 1999. Since its publication, the book has been added to the curriculum of high school classes and African-American and women's studies programs in colleges around the world.[clv] The Delany sisters' work is a great example that shows what is possible when you're committed to doing something.

Now consider some of the most memorable examples of those who accomplished great things at different ages against the odds.

- Helen Keller became deaf and blind at 19 months, and she later was the first deaf and blind person to earn a bachelor of arts degree.

- Mozart was already competent on keyboard and violin when he began composing at the age of 5.

- Magnus Carlsen became a chess grandmaster at the age of 13.

- Soccer superstar Pele, at 17, was the youngest player to play in a World Cup Final, the youngest scorer in a World Cup Final, and the youngest player to win a World Cup Winner's Medal.

- John Lennon was 20 and Paul McCartney was 18 when the Beatles had their first concert in 1961.

- Jesse Owens was 22 when he won four gold medals in Berlin in 1936.

- Beethoven was a piano virtuoso by age 23.

- Isaac Newton, at 24, wrote *Philosophiæ Naturalis Principia Mathematica.*

- Roger Bannister was 25 when he broke the four-minute mile record.

- Albert Einstein was 26 when he wrote the theory of relativity.

- Michelangelo created two of the greatest sculptures, *David* and *Pieta*, by age 28.

- Alexander the Great by age 29 had created one of the largest empires of the ancient world.

- Amelia Earhart was 31 when she became the first woman to fly solo across the Atlantic Ocean.

- Oprah Winfrey was 32 when she started her talk show, which became the highest-rated program of its kind.

- Edmund Hillary was 33 when he became the first man to reach the top of Mount Everest (the highest mountain in the world).

- Martin Luther King, Jr. was 34 when he delivered his *I Have a Dream* speech.

- Marie Curie was 35 when she was nominated for the Nobel Prize in Physics in 1903.

- The Wright brothers, Orville, 32, and Wilbur, 36, invented and built the world's first successful airplane and made the first controlled, powered, and sustained heavier-than-air human flight.

- Vincent Van Gogh was 37 when he died and was virtually unknown, yet his paintings are worth millions today.

- Neil Armstrong was 38 when he became the first man to set foot on the moon.

- Mark Twain was 40 when he wrote *The Adventures of Tom Sawyer* and 49 when he wrote *Adventures of Huckleberry Finn*.

- Christopher Columbus was 41 when he discovered the Americas.

- Rosa Parks was 42 when she refused to obey the bus driver's order to give up her seat to make room for a white passenger.

- John F. Kennedy was 43 when he became president of the United States.

- Henry Ford was 45 when the first Model T was produced.

- Suzanne Collins was 46 when she wrote *The Hunger Games*.

- Charles Darwin was 50 when his book *On the Origin of Species* was published.

- Leonardo da Vinci was 51 when he painted the *Mona Lisa*.

- Abraham Lincoln was 52 when he became president of the United States.

- Ray Kroc was 53 when he bought the first McDonald's franchise and took it to unprecedented levels.

- Dr. Seuss was 54 when he wrote *The Cat in the Hat*.

- Chesley "Sully" Sullenberger III was 57 when he successfully performed an emergency landing for US Airways Flight 1549 into the Hudson River in 2009. All of the 155 passengers aboard the aircraft survived.

- Colonel Harland Sanders was 61 when he started the KFC Franchise.

- J. R. R. Tolkien was 62 when the *Lord of the Rings* series was published.

- Ronald Reagan was 69 when he became president of the United States.

- Jack LaLanne, at age 70, while handcuffed and shackled, towed 70 rowboats.

- Nelson Mandela was 76 when he became president of South Africa.

Strategy

Now that you have plenty of examples to go by, let's look at the second cornerstone of living your purpose, which is having a strategy. A strategy is a plan of action or policy designed to achieve a major or overall aim. The reason for a strategy is to deal with the routines of day to day operations as you live your purpose. This is important because during your day to day attempts at living your purpose, your strategy will always be tested. For example, there will always be something that comes up that you didn't plan or didn't anticipate would happen. You can never plan for a life crisis or health problems or even the loss of a loved one. Your strategy is the component that keeps you on task to continue to live your purpose during those stressful phases in your life.

One of my favorite models to look at when it comes to planning my strategy is the work of the ant. Ants have routines for dealing with day to day operations, but they must always have ways of breaking those routines when faced with disturbances or unexpected circumstances. According to *National Geographic*, there are more than ten thousand known ant species around the world, and they all have a different way of adapting to their surroundings. According to the research article titled, "Traits Underlying the Capacity of Ant Colonies to Adapt to Disturbance and Stress Regimes," low temperatures, low nest site, and food resource availability are important stresses that affect ant abundance and distribution. Also, large-scale habitat disturbances, such as fire, grazing and mining, and small-scale disturbances that more directly affect individual colonies, such as predation, parasitism, and disease, also affect ant abundance and distribution.[clvi]

Ants communicate and cooperate by using chemicals, such as pheromones, which can alert others to danger or lead them to a promising food source. Consider the words of arguably the wisest person to ever live, King Solomon, who mentioned in 1 Kings 4:29, "And God gave him very great wisdom and understanding, and knowledge as vast as the sands of the seashore."[clvii] (KJV) King Solomon said this about the ant in Proverbs 6:6–8: "Go to the ant, thou sluggard; consider her ways, and be wise, which having no guide, overseer, or ruler, provideth her meat in the summer, and gathereth her food in the harvest." (KJV) King Solomon was advising us to consider the ways of the ant and to learn their strategy. And based on research of the ant and my personal experience, here are four strategies that I discovered in order to not only survive the unexpected circumstances of life, but to also live my purpose with a unified strategy for success. I called these the four P strategies of the ant. I hope these four strategies are able to help you like they've helped me to see the proof in living my purpose. **The four P strategies of the ant to survive the unexpected are performance, partnership, preparation, and perseverance.**

Performance

The first strategy that caught my attention about the ant concerns their performance. Sometimes it is really easy to mistake a lot of activity for success. Hall of Fame basketball coach John Wooden said, "Don't mistake activity with achievement." When it comes to ants, they don't ever mistake activity with achievement because they know they must perform to a certain level in order to survive and protect their colony. Ants are strong and hardworking insects for their size. They are noted for carrying objects that are much bigger than they are. A worker ant can lift an object weighing five to ten times its own weight and can drag an object twenty to fifty times heavier, whereas humans can rarely lift their own weight. However, ant muscles are no stronger than human muscles (in terms of force per cm^2), but the small size of ants (one to five milligrams) gives them an advantage as to how much muscle force they can produce.[clviii] It seems like they are not afraid of a heavy task because they seem to take pleasure in moving these objects to their colony.

As you're reading this book, I hope that you have your purpose and other goals that you want to accomplish in life. The purpose and your goals that you want to accomplish can seem huge and may appear much bigger than what you think you can handle. If you set them so high that they seem unattainable, then you'll only end up frustrated and discouraged in the process. Always remember the performance of the ant. The ant strategy reminds me of the saying, "Where there's a will, there's a way." Just thinking about how the ant tackles seemingly impossible tasks should encourage you to have a mindset that understands what is possible for you when it comes to living your purpose. It's important to focus on your performance.

Partnership

The second strategy that caught my attention related to ants is their desire to partnership with each other on their projects. Based on my findings, ants create partnerships and teamwork with each other. Everything an ant does is for the benefit of the entire colony. They work until they are done, and each ant is aware of their individual duty and does its part. There are more than 12,500 out of an estimated total of 22,000 species of ants that have been classified.[clix] And in each colony there are three kinds of ants that work together: soldier or worker ants, fertile male ants called drones, and one or more fertile females called queens. Ants show their partnership skills when it comes to the search for food. Some ants are tunneling and moving materials, and others may be looking for food. When an ant finds food, they'll mark a trail leading to the food source, which other ants will follow. Foraging ants travel distances of up to seven hundred feet from their nest, and scent trails allow them to find their way back even in the dark.[clx] In hot and arid regions, day-foraging ants face death by dehydration, so the ability to find the shortest route back to the nest reduces that risk. This partnership strategy is highly visible in the fire ant colony. Fire ants, named for their burning sting, possess incredible powers of flotation when they work together, turning themselves into life rafts that can survive flash floods in their native Brazilian rain forests and travel for months before making landfall.[clxi] The ants flounder in the water as individuals, so it's important that they work together. In terms of living your purpose, who is on your team?

Do you have individuals on your team who are concerned about your success? Now is the time to be sure you have the right partners on your team.

Preparation

The third strategy that we can learn from the ant is its desire to be prepared for the unexpected circumstances it might face on a daily journey. If ants had a vocabulary, I don't think the word procrastination would be a part of their language. Ants don't wait until the weather turns cold before they start storing food. They will gather food while the weather is still warm and take it to their colony. King Solomon reminded us of this in the book of Proverbs 6 and 30 respectively when he said, "Consider her ways and be wise, which, having no captain, overseer or ruler, provides her supplies in the summer, and gathers her food in the harvest," and, "There are four things [the rock badger, locust, lizard and ant] which are little on the earth, but they are exceedingly wise: The ants are a people not strong, yet they prepare their food in the summer."

King Solomon is referring to the preparedness of the ant. They are looking to the future each day and preparing for what lies ahead. An ant's life span is normally only about ninety days, but it depends on the environment, the type of ant, and other factors. Harvester ants seem to live a little longer, usually two to six months.[clxii] Ants usually do not have a long life expectancy, so all ants live for the same goal, to ensure by any means that their families live on. Is there something you should be doing to prepare to live your purpose? If so, consider the preparedness of the ant. Don't put it off! And, of course, always be prepared to live your purpose.

Perseverance

And the last strategy that I've learned from the ant is the art of perseverance. Ants have an amazing ability to survive all types of situations and all kinds of weather. Have you ever thought about the last time you tried to destroy their colony? I'm amazed that if I run over their colony while I'm mowing my lawn, by the next day the colony seems to be back just the way it was. They recover quickly and the damage is repaired seemingly in an instant. Ants persevere through danger, disaster, and disturbances. You can run over their anthill with a lawn mower, you can kick their anthill, or even wash it away with a water hose, and they're going to build it back as quickly as possible. Do you have that type of perseverance when it comes to your purpose? When it seems like no one believes in what you're trying to accomplish, will you persevere or will you give up? The ant uses a great strategy, which must be used when it comes to living your purpose. Legendary Hall of Fame football coach Vince Lombardi was noted for making historical statements. One of my favorite statements that reminds me of perseverance is when he said, "The price of success is hard work, dedication to the job at hand, and the determination that whether we win or lose, we have applied the best of ourselves to the task at hand." So based on the efforts of the ant and the wisdom of Lombardi, it's important to persevere as you live your purpose to fulfill your hopes, dreams, and aspirations.

Feedback

Now that you have plenty of examples to go by and a strategy to help you implement it, let's look at the third and final cornerstone of living your purpose, which is evaluating feedback. According to Merriam-Webster, feedback is defined as helpful information that is given to someone to say what can be done to improve a performance, a product, or an outcome.[clxiii] When it comes to feedback, it can be hard to receive when it doesn't sound good or feel good, but we need to hear it for our own good. This type of feedback normally occurs when failure is involved. Feedback comes in all shapes, forms, and sizes. For example, your grade on a test in school or college, the amount of weight you lose while on your diet or the amount of time and money it is estimated or expected to take to build your dream home. Feedback is used to keep you on schedule to accomplish what you desire. Feedback also can involve the celebration of a moment of an accomplishment or immediate course correction. For instance, actor Bruce Gordon gave a great example about feedback when he said, "Whatever you choose to do, you'll end up playing in one game or another. You may play a corporate game, an education game, or a health game. You can play any game, but if you want to be successful, you need to understand the rules and the intricacies of that game. Take it seriously because it's a serious game." And what game is Gordon referring to? I believe he's referring to the game of life. The feedback you get will direct you as to how you could make the proper adjustments that you need in order to get your desired results. Remember that feedback doesn't always need to have a negative or critical undertone, but it is important that you have it. **In order to understand and apply your feedback, you'll need to do the following: identify your feedback, understand characteristics of good feedback, and then decide what you will do with the feedback you've received.**

Identify your feedback

How do you identify feedback? The best way to identify feedback is to evaluate your results. For example, if you want to know what you earned on a test in a biology class, just look at your score or the grade you got on the test. That's your result. Or if you wanted to know if that stranger in the mall will say yes to going out with you on a date, your result will show when you ask the question. And sometimes, like in both of the previous scenarios, you might be afraid of the results because you're not prepared to deal with them. But I've learned that when it comes to using any feedback, I must buck up and take it like an adult. The feedback you get is the best tool or information that you can use in order to get your desired results in the future. The best and most simple way to identify feedback is to know that your results will either be identified as a success or as a failure. And sometimes, I really think that as human beings, we overanalyze what our results mean. Don't ever try to overanalyze and misconstrue the results to make yourself feel better about what the results say. For example, if you had not studied for the biology test and scored a fifty percent on it, you might blur the results in order to hear what you want to hear by saying something like, "There was a lot of information on that biology test that we didn't go over in class," or "The stuff on that test wasn't in our notes," or "The teacher made that test hard so that no one in class would pass." Whenever you misinterpret your feedback, you will never get the truth. The true feedback on that test says, "You need to study and be sure that you understand the information you're studying." Consider a situation when you're thinking about asking a classmate to go out on a date with you. The only way you'll get your results is by asking the question. And whatever the answer is to that question, would you be able to use that feedback to help you the next time you want to ask someone out? I would think so. The point is you need to identify your feedback, and don't make it say what it doesn't say. When you see your feedback as the truth, it will set you free.

Understanding characteristics of good feedback

After identifying your feedback, you'll need to understand the characteristics of good feedback. I believe that good feedback should be continuous and in the present; it should be specific and not general; and it should focus on building strengths rather than highlighting weaknesses. And by focusing those characteristics, your convictions will be stronger than your fears. You'll be able to focus on facts rather than opinions. And more importantly, you'll develop your self-esteem rather than self-protection. A synthesis of research literature led to the following characteristics, which validate good feedback. These characteristics were adapted from D. J. Nicol and D. Macfarlane-Dick.[clxiv] Good feedback practices help to clarify what good performance is (goals, criteria, and expected standards); facilitate the development of self-assessment (reflection); provide high-quality information to the participant; encourage dialogue; encourage positive motivational beliefs and self-esteem; provide opportunities to close the gap between current and desired performance; and provide information that can be used for future experiences.

Reaction to the feedback you've received

Once you know how to identify feedback and you have some understanding about the characteristics of good feedback, you will come to the last and probably most important part of the process. What will you do with the feedback that you've gained? You'll need to accept the fact that the feedback that you receive will be the truth. The truth is the best feedback you can use to generate change, but you have to accept it. Former Prime Minister Winston Churchill argued, "Men occasionally stumble over the truth, but most of them pick themselves up and hurry off as if nothing ever happened." Feedback is nothing more than the truth. But in order to prove your purpose, you must do something different after being exposed to the truth. It's amazing how most of us can read the writing on the wall (feedback and truth), but we just assume that it is addressed to someone else.

Know that you first have the responsibility to take care of yourself. If you've ever traveled on an airplane and you've heard all the safety instructions from the flight attendant during the safety demonstration, you know they emphasize that you should care for yourself first if an emergency arises. I can almost recite the announcement of the flight attendant word for word, "Oxygen and the air pressure are always being monitored. In the event of a decompression, an oxygen mask will automatically appear in front of you. To start the flow of oxygen, pull the mask towards you. Place it firmly over your nose and mouth, secure the elastic band behind your head, and breathe normally. Although the bag does not inflate, oxygen is flowing to the mask. **If you are travelling with a child or someone who requires assistance, secure your mask first, and then assist the other person.**" Greek philosopher Epictetus said it best when he said, "God has entrusted me with myself." Therefore, when you get any feedback, see what YOU must do for yourself first to correct or alter purpose before you assist anyone else.

You must decide what you will do with all this new found wisdom and experience. Consider the following four things you should do with any feedback that you receive. It doesn't matter what area of your life, you can apply this personally, professionally, or spiritually. This is going to take patience, perseverance, and self-awareness, so you must apply these actions every single day of your life. **The four responses to feedback are prepare yourself mentally for the results, take responsibility, adjust your course of action, and accept the feedback appropriately.** These four items will hopefully help you on your journey.

Mental Preparation. The first thing you must do even before you receive any feedback is to prepare yourself mentally. You have to be mentally tough to deal with any results that may come your way. The thought about being mentally tough came to mind when I was reading about giraffes. The giraffe is the tallest living animal, and its chief distinguishing characteristics are its extremely long neck and legs and its distinctive coat patterns. It stands sixteen to twenty feet tall and has an average weight of thirty-five hundred pounds for males and eighteen hundred pounds for females.[clxv] Now, think about the birth of a baby giraffe. According to Giraffe Conservation

Foundation, giraffes give birth standing up, requiring the newborn to fall just under six and a half feet to the ground! Designed for such an abrupt entry into the world, a newborn calf can stand up and run within an hour of being born.[clxvi] A baby giraffe is born in such a way that they are mentally (and physically) tough upon arrival. What about the birth of a wildebeest in Africa? How much time does it have after birth to learn how to run with the pack so it's not eaten by the lions, the hyenas, and all the other animals that are hunting them? Only a few minutes! As soon as a little wildebeest is born, it tries to stand up, only to keep falling until its small legs are strong enough to stand. When finally standing, and shaking on its weak legs, it tries to nurse. Only to be repeatedly pushed away by the mother. Why would the mother send this message? The message being sent says, "You don't have time to nurse now, you've got to develop some strength in your legs to get strong, or the lions and hyenas will get you. We don't have much time."

What about you? Do you have time to sit around and wait to get stronger in your purpose? Do you have time to wait for others to nurse you to health to become your best? Can you look back over your life to find something that showed you had been mentally prepared beforehand? If you have been mentally prepared in the past, use that experience and also the experience of others to help you become stronger. The road to success and the road to failure are almost exactly the same; the difference is in how you think about or respond to the results. William Shakespeare insisted that nothing was either good or bad but thinking made it so. We all have that little voice in the back of our mind that tells us to stop, or it won't work, or to just give up. Mentally tough people train that voice so that in times of difficulty it says, "Shut up; it'll work; don't give up," in much the same way the Navy Seals train themselves by thinking, "The only easy day was yesterday." President Thomas Jefferson said that nothing on earth could stop the man with the right mental attitude from achieving his goal, and nothing on earth can help the man with the wrong mental attitude. Do you think you're a mentally tough person? This is a question I ask myself every day. Sometimes I'm satisfied with the answer, and some days I know that the verdict is still out. Find different examples to show you how to be mentally tough.

Taking Personal Responsibility. The second thing to do with any feedback that you get is to take 100 percent personal responsibility for your actions. Botanist and inventor George Washington Carver said that ninety-nine percent of all failures come from people who have a habit of making excuses. Even though Carver was born into slavery, he went on to become one of the most prominent scientists and inventors of his time, as well as a teacher at the Tuskegee Institute. Carver devised more than 100 products using one of these crops—the peanut—including dyes, plastics and gasoline.[clxvii] I believe that Carver's success proves that when you take responsibility for your own actions, and not the actions of others, then you're able to accomplish great things. Self-help author and motivational speaker Wayne Dyer insisted that, "All blame is a waste of time. No matter how much fault you find with another, and regardless of how much you blame him, it will not change you." Not taking personal responsibility is just like looking in the mirror and seeing someone else. Irish playwright George Bernard Shaw said, "We are made wise not by the recollection of our past, but by the responsibility for our future." When we are faced with feedback that is 100 percent true, we must take action to do what we need to do with it. For if we don't, we'll be just like the description in James 1:23–25.

> "Anyone who listens to the word but does not do what it says is like someone who looks at his face in a mirror and, after looking at himself, goes away and immediately forgets what he looks like. But whoever looks intently into the perfect law that gives freedom and continues in it—not forgetting what they have heard, but doing it—they will be blessed in what they do (NIV)."

So just know that eventually, everyone will have to accept full and total responsibility for their actions, which means everything we have done and everything we have not done. I'd rather take the responsibility now.

Adjusting Your Course of Action. The third thing to do with any feedback that you get is to either change your course of action or remain full steam ahead. Of course, if you're not getting the results you desire from your feedback, evaluate what you're actually getting out of the process and tweak your plan of action. If you're getting your desired results from your feedback, consider remaining full steam ahead. Probably the most important aspect on this point is that you must remain flexible, and always be ready to make a decision about your next move. President John F. Kennedy said, "There are costs and risks to a program of action, but they are far less than the long-range risks and costs of comfortable inaction." When you're constantly getting feedback, don't get comfortable in your process. You never know when you'll have to slow down or come to a stop. If you're struggling with whether to change your course of action or remain full steam ahead, come up with a checklist. Use these adapted guidelines from Leandecisions.com for creating your decision checklist:[clxviii]

- **Set Your Priorities** Ask yourself, "What are the top three things that matter?" and then develop your questions around those.

- **Ask Yes/No Questions** Create clear criteria for whether an option should be considered.

- **Keep It Short** Aim for three to seven questions. Long checklists can seem daunting and are more likely to have irrelevant questions. Force yourself to limit the number of questions as a way of focusing on what's really important.

- **Mark Critical Questions** If a question must have a "yes" for the option to be considered, mark it as required. Put these questions near the top of your list.

- **Put Stricter Questions First** Reduce the number of questions that an option has to go through before being eliminated by putting the strictest questions first. If an option doesn't satisfy this question, then the other questions don't need to be asked.

- **Review Periodically Review** your checklist periodically to ensure the questions remain relevant for your decisions. Then look for new questions you should be asking. Update your checklist as needed.

Having a checklist to evaluate your progress will help you ensure you're asking all the right questions. Austrian-born management consultant, educator, and author Peter Drucker, was a leader in the development of management education, and he invented the concept known as management by objectives.[clxix] Drucker maintained that, "The most serious mistakes are not being made as a result of wrong answers. The truly dangerous thing is asking the wrong question."

Appropriate Acceptance. And the last thing to do with any feedback that you get is to accept the feedback for what it is, and maintain faith in what you're trying to accomplish. I believe that faith will not always get us what we want, but it'll definitely get what God wants for us. Take for instance the example of sixty-one-year-old potato farmer Cliff Young, who is probably not even known outside of Australia. The reason Young's story is so fascinating is because of what he was attempting to do and the feedback that he received as he attempted to accomplish this goal.

Each year, Australia hosts a 544-mile endurance race from Sydney to Melbourne that is probably one of the most grueling running races in the world. A race like this is only attempted by world-class athletes because this race takes about eight days to complete. In 1983, Young showed up at the start of this endurance race wearing overalls and works boots. If you were a spectator, you probably would have thought that he was also a spectator coming to cheer on the racers. But to everyone's amazement, Young picked up his race number at the registration table and joined in with the other 150 runners at the start gate. As the audience, the press reporters, and other athletes looked on with shock and dismay, they were probably thinking that there was no way he could win this race, or maybe even, there was no way that he would be able finish the race. They thought it was a crazy publicity stunt, but they realized this was real when he pinned his number to his overalls and moved into the pack of runners dressed in their expensive racing outfits. The camera focused on him and a reporter interviewed him.[clxx]

Reporter: "Who are you and what are you doing?"

Young: "I'm Cliff Young. I'm from a large ranch where we run
sheep outside of Melbourne."

Reporter: "Are you really going to run in this race?"

Young: "Yeah."

Reporter: "Got any backers?"

Young: "No."

Reporter: "Then you can't run."

To everyone who had any questions about his desire to compete and finish
the race, he replied, "Yes, I can. See, I grew up on a farm where we couldn't
afford horses or tractors, and the whole time I was growing up, whenever
the storms would roll in, I'd have to go out and round up the sheep. We
had two thousand sheep on two thousand acres. Sometimes I would have
to run those sheep for two or three days. It took a long time, but I'd always
catch them. I believe I can run this race."clxxi

Criticism from his competitors and the press insisted that he was too old,
he didn't have the right training, he was inexperienced, and he didn't have
the right sports apparel. And there were probably other reasons people
didn't believe in his ability to finish the race. I believe that Young accepted
that criticism for what it was, but he didn't let it deter him from something
he wanted to do.

When the race started, all the other racers quickly left Young behind as he
appeared to leisurely shuffle in his unorthodox running style, but it allowed
him to conserve energy. In a race of this magnitude, runners had to run
about eighteen hours a day and sleep the remaining six hours. Even though
this was important information, no one bothered to tell Young. He didn't
stop the first day nor the second day, even though he was being left behind
during the day time. He eventually made up for it during the night when all
the other runners were asleep. And it was on the last day as everyone slept
that Young passed his competition. And by the time the other runners
awoke, Young was too far ahead for anyone to catch him. And not only did

Young win the race, but he beat the record by two days, and the second place runner was more than nine hours behind him. Young finished the race in less than six days. When asked about how he had run the race without any sleep, he said, "I imagined I was chasing sheep and trying to outrun a storm."[clxxii] Young believed he was qualified to run this race because he had grown up on a sheep ranch, and as a kid on a sheep farm without horses or tractors, when a storm came, he had to round up the sheep that were scattered over two thousand acres. Young realized that his faith was already proven; he knew what was possible for him to do because he had already been doing it. The only difference was he had to do it a little longer than before, but he believed in what he was doing.

In conclusion, remember the three mechanisms of living your purpose, which I compared to a three-legged stool. These are called the three Ps of living your purpose: passion, practice, and proof. The stool is supported by all of the legs, so if one leg is weaker the stool will fall over. Therefore, all three legs are needed to support the stool, and in the same way, all three mechanisms are needed to support your purpose in order to live your purpose. As minister, educator, scholar, and social activist Benjamin Mays said:

> "It must be borne in mind that the tragedy of life doesn't lie in not reaching your goal. The tragedy lies in having no goal to reach. It isn't a calamity to die with dreams unfulfilled, but it is a calamity not to dream. It is not a disaster to be unable to capture your ideal, but it is a disaster to have no ideal to capture. It is not a disgrace not to reach the stars, but it is a disgrace to have no stars to reach for. Not failure, but low aim is sin."[clxxiii]

Hence, go and live your purpose to the fullest. Know that you have a purpose. Know that you can live your purpose. Know that you can dream your purpose. And how do I know? Because I'm living my purpose right now. I grew up as a young man wanting to play professional basketball. My athletic journey allowed me to make a variety of stops along the way. I was able to use basketball as an avenue to get a college education. Not only that, it led me to an opportunity to become an assistant basketball coach, which encouraged and motivated me to pursue a master's degree. And upon completing my master's degree, it allowed me an opportunity to become an assistant dean of student affairs, which motivated me to pursue a doctoral degree. And upon completion of the Ph.D., my true purpose and passion as a writer and speaker eventually rose to the surface.

I wrote the above to say this: Now that you have learned how to discover, define, and begin living your purpose with the information from this book, you can make a lasting impact on your family, your community, and your world. But most importantly, you'll make a lasting impact on your legacy. It is my hope that the time you have invested in reading this book has yielded you a return on knowledge, wisdom, and insight for your life's purpose. Your deeper purpose will continue to rise to the surface as you continue to move through each phase of your life. I'm thankful for all of my life experiences up to this point because those experiences are proof that anyone can discover their purpose, define their purpose, and most importantly, live their purpose. So now it's your turn! Today is a great day to start living your purpose.

Conclusion

Without commitment, you can't have depth in anything worth having, whether it's a relationship, a business, a hobby, or, most important, your purpose. So, if it rains on your parade, still be committed! If you lose your best friend, be committed! If you lose your job, be committed! If the storms of life destroy your health, be committed! And even if you lose everything you own, be committed!

—Dr. Samuel Jones

NOW THAT YOU'VE completed this book, I hope you have some sense of your purpose. I also hope that you know how important your purpose means to your family, your community and your environment. And lastly, I hope that you have the faith, courage, and determination to live your purpose. Sometimes when we are so motivated and inspired, we can easily forget about the hard work that it will take to make the proper changes needed in order to get desired results. Let's review the process to *Live Life on Purpose.*

Purpose

Why are you here? Why are you wearing what you're wearing? Why do you talk the way you talk? Why do you live where you live? Why are you reading this book? Why? Why? Why? The question of why is a serious and very important question about anything you want to know. I'm learning more and more each day that the answer is not always the most important thing. The most important thing is that the questions are asked. And whenever you ask why, you're looking for the foundation or reason for something. One of the most powerful reasons is the reason to live. And sometimes you have to find that reason all by yourself. I believe that everyone has to find their own reason to live. For me, my reason to live is my God-given purpose, which is to change lives with His word. His word is true, and it is His word that has changed my life. That's my reason to get up every single day of my life, no matter what happened yesterday. Your reason should encourage you to glance back at the past, but to focus on today with the hopes of doing something new tomorrow. Sometimes reasons and purpose are not always clear; they can be uncertain and even unstable. But as long as you have the desire to keep moving ahead, you'll never be at a loss for action. I always try to encourage people to not complain about their road to success because it's bumpy, but to give thanks because they're no longer stuck in a rut. The road to success is always under construction because it's a constant work in progress.

And that's the way our lives are. We are always under construction, but we need to recognize that we need the work. If your purpose would appear to you without stress or without fight, then you probably wouldn't recognize it. And that's why everything happens for a reason and a purpose, and it serves you. Like I said at the beginning of this book, your purpose has power. I think about why I'm here on earth. I think about why I'm here in this country. And I think about why I'm here in Mississippi and here in my community. I know that I am here to make a difference. And the only way for me to make the greatest difference is to live my purpose. I don't have time to compare myself to anyone else. I don't have time to worry about what I don't have. I don't even have time to worry about what anyone else is doing. I know that time is not running out, but I do know that my life is. Have you ever thought about figuring out your age in days instead of years? If not, try it now. Multiply 365 times your age in years rounded to the nearest quarter. For simplicity, we'll disregard leap years in these calculations. At the time of the writing of this book, I am 14,235 days or 39 years old. When I think that I'm 14,235 days old, I realize that's a lot of days. This makes me wonder to myself, "What have I been doing?" And I also wonder how many days I wasted on the things that don't really matter.

For me, my purpose has allowed me to become more focused on how I spend my time. It makes me realize more and more each day that I have goals to accomplish. But those goals are not my focus. My focus is on who I will become in the pursuit of what I want to accomplish. Who you become is truly the factor that influences other people the most. Earning a college degree or buying your dream home or even landing your dream job is not what makes that lasting impression on the people around you. Your love for people over and above your love for those accomplishments is what makes the difference. It takes a conscious decision for you to know who you're going to be.

As I have shared, decision making is the process of deciding between two or more possible alternatives in order to get a solution to a problem. Chances are you probably didn't know or understand purpose when you began reading this book, but now you'll have to make a conscious decision as to how you'll use the information you've learned. The benefit of what we learn is the knowledge we have for use later in life. It took me thirty years to discover my purpose. I believe that I was always working towards my purpose, but I wasn't conscious of purpose at the time. Yes, I've accomplished quite a few things before identifying my purpose, but only through God's grace and the help of a lot of people who believed in me, even when I made mistakes. I've been able to get a college education, travel overseas to play professional basketball, work as a college administrator, author books, start my own business, and have a fourteen-year successful marriage. And some of the things that I'm most proud of is serving my church family as a deacon for twelve years and now as an ordained minister of the gospel. All of my successes, failures, and shortcomings allowed me to be able to receive revelations from God. No matter how much information and education that you get in life, always seek revelations from God. Revelations will help you fight the temptation to think that you're in control. As the Bible says in Proverbs 4:7, "Wisdom is the principal thing; therefore get wisdom. And in all your getting, get understanding." (NKJV) It is my hope that you gain an understanding about your purpose, and that you will make the right decision based on where you are in your life.

Now get up and stand on your feet. I have appeared to you to appoint you as a servant and as a witness of what you have seen and will see of me.

—Acts 26:16 (NIV)

Discover Your Purpose

When was the last time that something major happened in your life? Examples of major events could be the birth of a child, a loved one graduating from high school or college, the purchase of a new automobile or a new home, or even the loss a loved one. All of these are examples of things that happen every single day that can give us great joy or great sorrow. The question is, though, how will you allow them to help you discover something about yourself? All of these events serve to remind you to cherish each moment of life and to help you discover your purpose. I shared with you how I solidified my purpose in the pulpit when I accepted the call into the ministry to preach and teach God's word. I share that example because I was already on the path to doing it. It just took time for me to get there. And that could be the same for you. You're probably already on the path to finding your purpose. I hope this book will encourage you to stay on the road and to not take anything for granted, and to experience everything in life with your eyes, heart, soul, and mind open. And was earlier mentioned, you'll have to do four things: overcome fear, expose yourself to positive messages, raise your standards of thought, and focus.

Overcome Fear

Remember that fear is false expectations appearing real. Whenever you're doing something new, it's always going to be uncomfortable, scary, and uneasy. But if you continue to do new things, the constant fear will begin to subside. The only true way to cure the fear of doing something is to do it.

And each time you do it, your confidence will grow, and your fear will be destroyed little by little. The story about David and Goliath in the Bible reminds me to speak positive words to myself as I face the giants in my own life. Here is my summarized version of the story, but you can read it in 1 Samuel 17.

The Philistine army had gathered for war against Israel, and they faced each other camped on opposite sides of a steep valley. A Philistine giant named Goliath, measuring more than nine feet tall and wearing full armor came out each day for forty days, mocking and challenging the Israelites to fight. Saul, the King of Israel, and his army were terrified of Goliath. And then one day, a young man was sent to the battle lines by his father to check on his brothers. When David got there, he realized that his brothers were okay, but he also heard this giant shouting his threats and saw the army of Israel was filled with great fear. Upon hearing these threats from the giant and seeing the fear of the army, David volunteered to fight this giant. David killed Goliath in what seemed to be an unmatched battle, but his belief in God allowed him to prevail.

But I'm more interested in what David told himself as he prepared to fight Goliath. As David prepared himself for battle, he penned these words in Psalm 23: "Yea, though I walk through the valley of the shadow of death, I will fear no evil; for you are with me; your rod and your staff, they comfort me." (NKJV) What words will you write to yourself when you're faced with your own Goliath? What words will you say to yourself when you come to a point in life when you don't know what to do? I prefer to follow the example of David when he said, "I will fear no evil, for you are with me." When overcoming fear, we must know that God is with us. And once we know God is with us, our giants won't seem so big.

Expose Yourself to Positive Messages

You will become the messages that you hear the most and the messages you believe the most. I found two principle ways to expose myself to positive messages that have helped me to discover my purpose. The first principle was to control the messages that I chose to believe based on my own thoughts, remarks from others, or the messages that are communicated from the environment that I'm in. The second principle way I exposed myself to positive messages in order to discover my purpose was to consistently seek out positive messages. I would encourage you to expose yourself, your children, your family, and your friends to different things that will provoke deep thoughts. Most of the time, we like to stay within our comfort zone, but realize that our comfort zone doesn't challenge us to think, and when we're not thinking, we are more likely to miss the revelation of the message we need in order to be the change that makes a difference. And that difference is always your purpose.

Raise Your Standards of Thought

So how do you raise your standards of thought? According to Bertie Charles Forbes, the author who founded *Forbes Magazine*, you raise your standards of thought by changing what you concentrate on. He maintained that you are what you set out to be; you are a composite of the things you say, the books you read, the thoughts you think, the company you keep, and the things you desire to become. Aristotle maintained that choosing high intentions, sincere effort, and intelligent execution is what helps us to raise our standards of excellence with thought. I've found that when I raised my standards of thinking, I was able to discover my purpose. As the scripture says in Proverbs 23:7, "For as a man thinketh in his heart, so he is." (NKJV) The higher you are with your thinking, the clearer your vision for your purpose in life will become. So you are exactly who you think you are.

Focus, Focus, Focus

Did you know that you have an array of things that you can focus on every day? For example, here is just one thing that you could focus on for today: yourself, in terms of how you feel, how you look, how you think, how you act, how you respond to the past, how you react to the present and the future, what's right, what's wrong. And these are just things dealing with self. Just imagine how many things you could consider if you focused on other people. The point I'm trying to make is that we have so many other things that can take our attention off of the things that we should be focused on, like why did Johnny and Mary down the street get a divorce? Why didn't your best friend get that job? Why did the President of the United States take a selfie at Nelson Mandela's memorial service? Since there are so many things grabbing at your attention, I want to encourage you to narrow your focus onto the important things in life. When you narrow your focus, you change your frame of mind, which changes the course of your life. Therefore, understand four simple principles when it comes to focus: time, subject, message, and response. First, time is the only thing that we spend that we can't get a refund on, so spend it wisely. Spend time focusing on the right things. Secondly, no matter what the problem, your life is always the subject. Use your past experiences to discover what you're capable of handling. We have always been able to handle adversity; sometimes we just forget what we've already overcome with our most precious subject, our life. Thirdly, what message are you sending the universe when you focus? You're telling the universe that you think "this" (whatever you're focusing on) is important. Always remember that you're constantly sending messages to yourself and to others around you. When you focus, you're communicating to yourself and the universe what is important to you. And lastly, you'll have a response when you focus. No matter what happens in life, you'll always have to follow up with a response, and your response shows what type of results you want to have. Keep in mind, to shine the light on self-first, means to be sure we have the right intent in our heart. I'm always focusing on the actions of self-first, instead of focusing on the actions of other people. And when I do that, it helps me to keep my purpose at the center of my attention.

For I know the thoughts that I think toward you, says the Lord, thoughts of peace and not of evil, to give you a future and a hope. Then you will call upon me and go and pray to me, and I will listen to you. And you will seek me and find me, when you search for me with all your heart. I will be found by you, says the Lord, and I will bring you back from your captivity; I will

gather you from all the nations and from all the places where I have driven
you, says the Lord, and I will bring you to the place from which I caused you
to be carried away captive.

—*Jeremiah 29:11–14 (NKJV)*

Discover the Intelligent Purpose

If you're going to build your purpose on something, make sure that your foundation is solid, stable, and can stand the test of life. The foundation for your purpose should always be built upon overcoming your fears, constantly exposing yourself to positive messages, raising your standards of thought and continuing to focus on the things that will bring you the results you desire. Then it will be time to move to the next phase of building your purpose by analyzing your abilities and talents and by identifying your learning styles, which I call the intelligent purpose. I call it the intelligent purpose because I believe that everyone has the capability to be logical, have clear well processed thoughts, be understanding, communicate with others, and learn. Your purpose should always reflect back to these elements because this is the foundation for your learning style and how you relate to other people.

Researchers refer to these learning styles and elements as intelligence. As previously mentioned, Howard Gardner defined intelligence as a biological and psychological potential to solve problems and to create products that are valued in one or more cultural contexts. Gardner suggested that there are multiple kinds of intelligence, and everyone has some form of intelligence. The key is to know what your intelligence area is and to focus on that area and to apply the principles to your behaviors. There are nine intelligences or talents[clxxiv]:

- Spatial intelligence—the ability to think in three dimensions. Core capacities include mental imagery, spatial reasoning, image manipulation, graphic and artistic skills, and an active imagination.

- Linguistic intelligence—the ability to think in words and to use language to express and appreciate complex meanings. Linguistic intelligence allows us to understand the order and meaning of words and to apply meta-linguistic skills to reflect on our use of language.

- Logical intelligence—the ability to calculate, quantify, consider propositions and hypotheses, and carry out complete mathematical operations. It enables us to perceive relationships and connections and to use abstract, symbolic thought, sequential reasoning skills, and inductive and deductive thinking patterns.

- Bodily intelligence—the capacity to manipulate objects and use a variety of physical skills. This intelligence also involves a sense of timing and the perfection of skills through mind–body union.

- Musical intelligence—the capacity to discern pitch, rhythm, timbre, and tone. This intelligence enables us to recognize, create, reproduce, and reflect on music, as demonstrated by composers, conductors, musicians, vocalists, and sensitive listeners.

- Interpersonal intelligence—the ability to understand and interact effectively with others. It involves effective verbal and nonverbal communication, the ability to note distinctions among others, sensitivity to the moods and temperaments of others, and the ability to entertain multiple perspectives.

- Intrapersonal intelligence—the capacity to understand ourselves and our thoughts and feelings, and to use such knowledge in planning and directing one's life. Intrapersonal intelligence involves not only an appreciation of the self, but also of the human condition.

- Naturalistic intelligence—designates the human ability to discriminate among living things (plants, animals) as well as sensitivity to other features of the natural world (clouds, rock configurations).

- Existential intelligence—showing sensitivity and the capacity to tackle deep questions about human existence, such as the meaning of life, why do we die, and how did we get here.

Remember, everyone has some form of the nine talents described above but it's up to you to figure out which one best fits your skill set. Get out there and discover what your passion is. When you put a limit on what you will do, you're putting a limit on what you can do.

Only be strong and very courageous, that you may observe to do according to all the law which Moses my servant commanded you; do not turn from it to the right hand or to the left, that you may prosper wherever you go. This Book of the Law shall not depart from your mouth, but you shall meditate in it day and night, that you may observe to do according to all that is written in it. For then you will make your way prosperous, and then you will have good success. Have I not commanded you? Be strong and of good courage; do not be afraid, nor be dismayed, for the Lord your God is with you wherever you go.
—Joshua 1:7–9 (NKJV)

Define Your Purpose

Purpose can be defined for any organization large or small. And if purpose can be defined for an organization as big as Wal-Mart, surely purpose can be defined for individuals who want to make a difference in their own life and in the lives of others. In order for individuals to define their purpose, they should begin by applying discipline in several major areas. You can define your purpose by being disciplined with your thinking, by taking risks, and by challenging your own belief system.

Thinking

One of the most life-changing revelations I've had is that I can do something about my thoughts. I don't have to mediate on everything that comes to my mind. I can choose what to think about, how much to think about it, and what I will do after spending time and effort thinking about it. Apostle Paul gave us valuable instructions about our thinking in Colossians 3:2 when he said, "Set your mind on things above, not on things on the earth." (NKJV) In Romans 12:2, Paul again instructed, "And do not be conformed to this world, but be transformed by the renewing of your mind, that you may prove what is that good and acceptable and perfect will of God." (NKJV) Paul is telling us to think about things that are spiritual, or things important to God (the higher things), and in doing so we will always fill our minds with good, honorable thoughts. And he is also telling us that if we want to know what God's perfect will is for our life or our purpose, then we must be transformed with a renewed mind. The only way to renew our minds is with our thinking.

Take Risks

Do you like to take risks or do you like to play it safe? If you're like me, then it really depends on what there is to lose versus what there is to gain. Just know that your reward will determine how much you are willing to risk. Are you willing to risk changing your life to live your purpose? Before you answer that question, you must first recognize what areas of your life need to change. I can't tell you all the areas of your life that you can change, but I can tell you that you'll have to take a risk and change your habits. If you plan to stay in your comfort zone, then you're taking a bigger risk by staying the same. And if you stay the same, you're dying and not growing. I would encourage you to take a bigger risk by doing something different because that's how you'll become different, which will make a difference. And as I said in the section on risk, whenever we're afraid of change, we've failed to realize that we've become kings and queens of our comfort zone. Today is a good day to denounce yourself from that throne (your comfort zone) because you don't put new wine into old wine skins. As motivational speaker Dennis Waitley insisted, "Life is inherently risky. There is only one big risk you should avoid at all costs, and that is the risk of doing nothing."

Challenge Your Belief System

How do people think differently and, in the process, allow themselves to behave differently? Why do we sometimes find it so easy to think differently and yet at other times we struggle? In order to think differently about anything, you have to start by challenging your own belief system. Naturally your belief system is characterized as a set of commonly supported and trusted ideas that you have learned and that you live by. How you view your life experiences determines the kind of belief system you have. And once you've formed a belief, you normally don't challenge it again unless you're forced to because your belief feels true to you. And if it feels like it's true, then it is true. So always challenge your personal belief system in order to find the whole truth, and not your version of the truth.

We all need to balance how to think differently with how to lessen our own personal biases. The reality is that in order to think differently we need to be good at thinking about challenging what we already believe. To think differently about what you already believe, you need to be conscious of where your intellectual and emotional energies are invested when your beliefs are challenged. When challenged, do you feel threatened? Do you take things personally? Do you feel entitled to what you already think? If these are your feelings when challenged, then your current belief system needs to change. But if you feel loved when challenged, or you feel that people are looking for the best idea when they challenge you, or you know not to take the challenge personally, then you're already challenging your current belief system. Of course, this takes constant practice and high emotional intelligence so know that you have what it takes. And just know that you'll be well on your way to defining your purpose.

Commit your works to the Lord, and your thoughts will be established.
—Proverbs 16:3 (NKJV)

Live Your Purpose

How do you live life on purpose? I believe that you must have three things in order to live life on purpose. I believe that you must have passion, you must practice what is important, and then you must consistently show proof of why you do what you do. As author Ralph Waldo Emerson maintained, "The purpose of life is not to be happy. It is to be useful, to be honorable, to be compassionate, and to have it make some difference that you have lived and lived well." So don't believe that you're here to be in competition with someone else. But know that you were put here to achieve your greatest self, to live out your purpose and to do it without fear. For even if you fear, you'll know that you're still alive and that what you're striving for is well worth it because fear only shows up to let you know that you're headed towards greatness.

Passion

Did you know that you sign your name every single day of your life? You sign your name to everything that you touch. You sign your name to every activity or task that someone asks you to complete. However, most people don't realize they are signing their name to everything they do. That's why it's important to have passion as one of your behaviors in order to live your purpose. Hall of Fame Coach Rick Pitino reminded me of this when he was coaching in the National Basketball Association for the Boston Celtics. As the head coach of the Celtics, he often had his players sign basketballs for charities or schools. The players would sign the ball and pass it around for everyone's signature and put the ball in a bag. Pitino removed a ball from the bag and noticed the ball had two indecipherable names written on it. And the way Pitino respond to his two players is how I want to respond. Pitino said:

> "You work all your life to get to this point where people want
> your autograph and nobody can read your signature. Every ounce
> of perspiration you left on the playground, every hour you put
> into footwork drills and conditioning and studying film—all of
> that was done to reach this level and play for the Boston Celtics.

Don't just scribble your name and number. Be proud of your name and number that you worked so hard to make valuable."clxxv

Pitino is saying take pride and show passion in everything that you do. And if you're really going to live your life with purpose, you must understand that this includes everything that you do. As Bishop T.D. Jakes encouraged, "If you don't know your purpose, follow your passion; for your passion will always lead to your purpose."

Practice

Did you know that everyone has great practice skills? We do, and I equate those practice skills to habits. Habits are just things that we unconsciously practice every day of our lives. If you're going to be better at doing anything in life, then be aware of the current habits you're practicing. Former college football coach Bobby Bowden insisted the greatest mistake is to continue to practice a mistake. Be mindful of what you're practicing, as this timeless riddle reminds us:

"I am your companion. I am your greatest helper or heaviest burden. I will push you onward or drag you down to failure. I am completely at your command. Half of the things you do you might just as well turn over to me and I will be able to do them quickly and correctly. I am easily managed—you must merely be firm with me. Show me exactly how you want something done and after a few lessons I will do it automatically. I am servant of all great men; and alas, of all failures, as well. Those who are great, I have made great. Those who are failures, I have made failures. I am not a machine, though I work with all the precision of a machine plus the intelligence of a man. You may run me for profit or run me for ruin—it makes no difference to me. Take me, train me, be firm with me, and I will place the world at your feet. Be easy with me and I will destroy you. Who am I? I am habit!"

—Anonymous

Proof

Can you now show the world your purpose? Hopefully, after getting to this point in the book, you're ready to show proof of your purpose. Do you have everything you need? Do you need to add any other ingredients to the pursuit of your purpose, perhaps perseverance? Do you need to add knowledge and expertise in some area to show proof of your purpose? Or do you need to add a mentor to your purpose process? Hopefully you'll be able to answer questions like these after you have some proof about what your true purpose is in life. You must be sure that you know who you are. Remember the old saying that inside every individual, there are six people who live there. And these six people tend to show up based on the given situation. The six people are: who you are reputed to be, who you are expected to be, who you were in the past, who you wish to be, who you think you are, who you really are. Since there are six people in all of us, consider using these three cornerstones, which have definitely made an impact on my life and how I live my life on purpose. **These cornerstones are examples, strategy, and feedback.**

Examples

There are at least two perfect ways that you can learn anything you want to learn. One way is trial and error. That means, try to do something, see what didn't work and try, try again. Or use the second way and learn from the examples of others who have gone before you. Prussian statesman Otto von Bismarck insisted, "Only a fool learns from his own mistakes. The wise man learns from the mistakes of others." So ask yourself, who out there is doing something you want to do? What is their background? How did they get started? What industry did they get started in? Of course these questions can go on and on. The point is, find some examples that will help you think outside of your knowledge zone. Sometimes you don't know what you don't know, but having some examples can help answer some of those questions, which you don't even know that you need to ask. These questions will help you focus on your outcomes instead of the obstacles that you might have to face.

Strategy

A strategy is just a well-defined way of organizing your resources in order to achieve your desired outcome. In terms of living your purpose, your strategy should be to organize your thinking. Your thoughts lead to actions, your actions lead to habits, your habits lead to your lifestyle, and your lifestyle will eventually lead to your legacy. You'll need to have a well-defined strategy that will keep you accountable every day. Below is a simple strategy I use in order to gauge the level of my thinking:

0% confidence and effort—I won't.

10% confidence and effort—I can't.

20% confidence and effort—I don't know how.

30% confidence and effort—I wish I could.

40% confidence and effort—I could.

50% confidence and effort—I think I might.

60% confidence and effort—I might.

70% confidence and effort—I think I can.

80% confidence and effort—I can.

90% confidence and effort—I will.

100% confidence and effort—I did.

—Author Unknown

Feedback

Do you really want to know what others think about your efforts? If you're concerned about your answer to that question, just know that a truthful evaluation of yourself gives feedback for continued growth and success. Feedback is just something that tells you how you're doing in certain areas of your life. It tells you how well you're doing, and it also tells you how you can improve in certain areas of your life. Feedback can be your best friend or your worst enemy; it just depends on how you look at it.

You make known to me the path of life; you will fill me with joy in your presence, with eternal pleasures at your right hand.

—*Psalm 16:11 (NIV)*

Final Thoughts

As I bring this book to a close, think about this topic of purpose and put yourself into this scenario: Imagine that your eyes are closed as you're reading the last few pages of this book. Then think about the last time you got your best rest. Was it when you fell asleep by the fireplace on a cold winter night as the flames of the fire flickered and the wood crackled? Or was it on a hot summer night after a nice long shower to wash away the heat of the day as the cold air from the air conditioner allowed you to drift away into a perfect rest? Or was it on a nice, cool spring afternoon with the birds chirping as a nice breeze was blowing while reading your favorite book as you laid in your hammock in the backyard? Whatever your favorite way is to fall asleep, just imagine that.

Also imagine that after reading this book, I just tapped you on your shoulder to wake you up. And as you wiped the sleep out of your eyes, you realized that you're on an airplane. And you have no idea about your travel arrangements. You don't know the travel itinerary. You don't know the time. You don't know if you are on your way to your final destination. You don't know anything about your trip. But there's one thing that you know as I stand with you through this sudden confusion: when we land, I'll give you some last minute travel advice as you board your final connecting flight to get you to where you have realized you need to go.

Now that you've completed *Live Life on Purpose*, and you are prepared for the final leg of your journey, I will send you on your way with these last words. First, by completing this book, you just received your first class ticket to your final destination: your purpose. It's waiting for you to arrive. Secondly, once you board the flight, there's no turning back. Since you've accepted the ticket by making yourself aware and conscious of the new information in this book, you can't turn back now. New results are only available by new awareness and choices. By reading this book, you have already made a commitment to live life on purpose whether you realize it or not. And thirdly, since all of your travel arrangements have been confirmed, just know that this final flight will be the beginning of a new day in your life because it's getting you to your purpose, which is your final destination. Living life on purpose is a continuous process and I'm proud to know that you've allowed me to travel this journey with you. Your destiny as defined in this scenario is your purpose in life. Or better yet, the reason why you are here on earth, the reason why you were born. This final part of your trip will mold you to become the person you've been created to be because you'll need to continue traveling with your purpose as a strongly defined part of your life. If that sounds intimidating, just remember that a journey of a thousand miles begins with one step and that each step takes time. And from the perspective of living life on purpose, your journey begins with one minute, one hour, one day in time:

60 seconds equals one minute

60 minutes equals one hour

24 hours equals one day

7 days equals one week

4 weeks on average equals one month

12 months equals one year

10 years equals one decade

10 decades equals one century

And since we all have time on our hands, I want to encourage you to use your time to live your purpose. And for me, it's only taken one action, one thought, or one smile for me to live life on purpose. And for you, it could take any one of these actions:

One memory can wake your dream,

One song from a bird can welcome spring;

One handshake can lift a soul,

One small accomplishment can score the goal,

One vote can change a nation,

One thought can welcome patience;

One candle can light a room,

One smile can conquer gloom;

One word must start each prayer,

One sincere touch shows how much you care;

One flower can start a garden,

One word of forgiveness and we're all pardoned;

One touch begins a friendship,

One sacrifice was the test of leadership;

One is blind and one can see,

One God to show it's me;

One heart to know it's true,

And at the end of the day, it's all up to you!

May your future be worthy of your purpose!

—Dr. Samuel Jones

Applying Live Life on Purpose

... to learn and not to do is really not to learn. To know and not to do is really not to know.

—Stephen Covey

Before you begin to apply *Live Life on Purpose*, answer the following question. What is your purpose in life?

_____

_____

_____

_____

_____

Now that you have your purpose strongly defined, how do you plan to put it into action? This is the one question to ask yourself as you come to the end of *Live Life on Purpose*. I'm going to offer a strategy to help you live life on purpose. Of course, this strategy is like anything else that you want to be

successful at: it's going to take focus, dedication, persistence, and consistency. I call this plan '30 Days to Live Life on Purpose.' Why thirty days?
Researchers have indicated that thirty days are essential when it comes to
applying new thoughts, ideas, and actions to your life. This theory was
formed and proven by researchers at NASA during an experiment with astronauts who were learning how to deal without gravity, particularly with
being upside down in space. The researchers were trying to determine the
effects of being in a weightless environment for long periods of time and
the effects the disorientations of space would have on astronauts and the
human mind.

NASA fit the astronauts with goggles that literally flipped their field vision
180 degrees. These astronauts even wore these goggles when they slept.
They saw everything upside down twenty-four hours a day, seven days a
week. And to the researchers' surprise, they found that after thirty days, the
astronauts' brains had completely flipped the image back so that everything
appeared normal even though they were still wearing the goggles. Their
brains had made new neuron networks to make the upside down world appear normal to the astronauts.

NASA continued to conduct this training, but the difference was that the
astronauts would be allowed to take the goggles off for short periods of
time. At the fifteen-day mark, they took off the goggles for one day.
However, for this group, the brain failed to make the same network adjustments. This one day without the goggles turned out to break the pattern
that the brain was making. This experiment confirmed to the researchers
that it takes thirty consecutive days to allow the brain to create new neuron
networks, which leads to new behavior.

Therefore, I encourage you to use this thirty day plan answering the daily
questions, preferably early in the day and then reflecting on your answers
before bed, for thirty consecutive days. And just like the NASA study, you
will not make the preferred progress if you're not consistent for the entire
thirty days. You'll have some flexibility in how you can approach your thirty
days. One way is just focus on each day's activity. For example, read only
the activity on Day 1, and then read only the activity on Day 2, and so on.

A second way your thirty day plan can be used, and I recommend this way, is to repeat each daily activity each day in order to reiterate the lessons learned. For example, on Day 2, review Day 1 and then move on to Day 2. And by Day 30, your reflection will be a review in order to keep it fresh in your mind daily. I highly recommend this thirty day plan be repeated, as needed, as a refresher once your purpose is established for several reasons. First, a life changing event such as a job change or death in the family could impact your purpose and change your previous answers. Secondly, as your purpose is modified by changes in life, so will your previous answers; it would be wise to monitor your progress. Thirdly, if for some reason you get off track while on the path of your purpose, a repeat of this plan can get you back in place. And fourth, like anything else, the more you practice something, the better at it you'll become. The more you repeat this plan, the better you will become at recognizing what's possible as you begin to get stronger in living your purpose. With consistency, your brain will rewire itself to accept this new information about your purpose. And, hopefully, after thirty days, this purpose consciousness will become a part of your permanent consciousness. By the end of thirty days, you'll become more like the person you were born to be, which will lead you to having the confidence you need in order to live life on purpose. Prepare for this new paradise in your mind.

Days 1–6 Purpose (Laying the foundation)—The foundation is the most important component of anything you build. Your purpose will only be as strong as your ability to reflect on the life experiences that have made you who you are. These first six days will assist you in laying a strong foundation on which your purpose will be built.

Day 1—Name three momentous events that occurred in your life and the most important lessons you learned from them. (If you have more than three events, please feel free to write them down with the lessons learned from each. Remember, these exercises are for you.)

_____

_____

_____

_____

_____

Day 2—What new decisions can you make from the previous life events and lessons learned that you listed on Day 1?

_____

_____

_____

_____

_____

Day 3—When you read the story of the life of Nelson Mandela in Chapter 1, what was the most important lesson you learned from his experience?

_____

_____

_____

_____

_____

_____

_____

Day 4—How can you apply the lessons learned from Mandela's experience to your life? Please be detailed in your answer.

_____

_____

_____

_____

_____

_____

_____

Day 5—When you read about the experiences of Victor Frankl in Chapter 1, what was the most important lesson you learned from his experience?

_____

_____

_____

_____

_____

_____

Day 6—How can you apply the lessons learned from Frankl's experience to your own life? Please be detailed in your reflections.

_____

_____

_____

_____

_____

_____

Days 7–12 Discover your purpose (A hidden treasure)—Your purpose is the hidden treasure that has been right before your eyes. A treasure is something that holds its value through the test of time. Your purpose is that treasure that will stand the test. In the next five days, you will discover the treasure that has been dormant. It's time for you to now put it on display.

Day 7—Since reading *Live Life on Purpose*, list at least five things you've learned about yourself, and describe how you might use them to help others.

_____

_____

_____

_____

_____

Day 8—Make a list of all your current fears, and the reasons behind the fears. How can you overcome those fears?

_____

_____

_____

_____

_____

Day 9—What were the most important lessons you learned from Joseph's experience as described in the section on exposure to positive messages in Chapter 2? How can you apply these lessons to your daily life?

_____

_____

_____

_____

_____

_____

Day 10—What lessons can you apply to your own life from J. K. Rowling's experience described in the section on acknowledgement/acceptance in Chapter 2?

_____

_____

_____

_____

_____

_____

Day 11—Reread Bruce Lee's letter to himself in Chapter 2, in the section "Raise your standards of thought." Write a letter to yourself similar to Lee's. Read your letter at least three times today.

_____

_____

_____

_____

_____

Day 12—Make a "Top Five" list of what's most important to you. How much time did you think about each one today, and what action did you perform to solidify your beliefs toward each item on your list? Describe how the items relate to your purpose.

_____

_____

_____

_____

_____

_____

Days 13–16 Discover your intelligent purpose (All things become new)—Who knows you better than you? In the next four days, you'll have a very exact idea about who you really are. And not only that, you'll be asked to evaluate how well you actually match up in action compared to who you say you are, and you'll be asked about your role models.

Day 13—Morning assignment: Describe yourself in five words or less. Evening assignment: Did you project yourself today in the way you described yourself?

_____

_____

_____

_____

_____

Day 14—Rank the nine talents described in Chapter 3 from your strongest to your weakest. How can you improve both your strengths and weaknesses in these areas?

_____

_____

_____

_____

_____

Day 15—What job/task/service would you do for free? Find a way to do that activity at least once a week.

_____

_____

_____

_____

_____

_____

Day 16—Who are your role models? What are their character traits that you admire most?

_____

_____

_____

_____

_____

_____

Days 17–23 Define your purpose (The true meaning)—When it comes to defining anything, it's really the idea of putting some parameters around the context of what you have. Over the next seven days, you'll be asked to put some parameters around your time, your behaviors and your thinking. The purpose of these next few days is to be sure that you're specific, intentional and strategic about your thinking and behaviors towards your purpose.

Day 17—List five ways that you spend your time that helps you pursue your purpose, and five ways that you spend your time that keeps you from pursuing your purpose.

_____

_____

_____

_____

_____

Day 18—List five behaviors that you can repeat each day that will help your purpose in life become part of your consciousness.

_____

_____

_____

_____

_____

Day 19—Since reading *Live Life on Purpose*, what has been your greatest discovery about your own way of thinking?

_____

_____

_____

_____

_____

_____

Day 20—Now that you have your purpose defined, what will be the greatest risk that you'll take in order to live life on purpose?

_____

_____

_____

_____

_____

_____

Day 21—Where else might you find guidance to help direct you towards your goal to live life on purpose? Be sure to include friends, family, coworkers, and other people in your purpose. How will you hold yourself accountable?

_____

_____

_____

_____

_____

Day 22—What are some beliefs that you had about yourself before reading *Live Life on Purpose*? What caused you to believe those things about yourself in the past? Have you changed your way of thinking?

_____

_____

_____

_____

_____

_____

Day 23—What are some new beliefs that you now have about yourself since reading *Live Life on Purpose?* Compare your results to Day 22.

_____

_____

_____

_____

_____

_____

Days 24–30 Live your purpose (Life on purpose)—As in biology, a living thing is a form of life composed in part of vital processes, which are capable of responding to stimuli, reproduction, growth and development. As compared to your purpose in life, your purpose must be able to sustain life in order to respond to your environment. These next seven days will inspire actions to live your purpose, which will also prove that your purpose is alive and well.

Day 24—Living things are composed of cells: What support do you need in order for your purpose to be self-sufficient? Are there programs or classes available to help you get constant feedback on the strengths and weaknesses of what you're doing with your purpose? Where are opportunities available for you to practice your purpose by volunteering your time?

_____

_____

_____

_____

Day 25—Living things have different levels of organization: What organizations, foundations, or agencies are out there that you can get involved with in order to help you organize how you apply/serve/activate your purpose?

_____

_____

_____

_____

Day 26—Living things use energy: What energy (efforts) can you apply that will help with the maintenance and growth of your purpose? What new classes can you take that will help you? What projects do you want to accomplish that you can throw your heart, soul, and spirit into?

_____

_____

_____

_____

_____

Day 27—Living things respond to their environment: How will you respond in your environment (home, friends, work, and community) to your current stimulus (your purpose)? Always remember that your current behavior is a complex set of responses to your current environment.

_____

_____

_____

_____

_____

Day 28—Living things grow: How can you grow the impact of your purpose? How can you touch more lives by living your purpose? How can your different levels of organization help you grow your purpose while you serve in order to meet those organizational needs? (Refer back to Day 25.)

_____

_____

_____

_____

_____

_____

Day 29—Living things adapt to their environment: What changes do you need to make to your current environment (home, friends, work, and community) that will support the growth of your purpose?

_____

_____

_____

_____

_____

_____

Day 30—Living things reproduce: Reproduction is not essential for the survival of an individual's life, but it must occur for your purpose to survive. What will you leave for future generations, who will never know you, in order for them to be affected by your purpose in life? What will your legacy say about your purpose in life? Will you use the time you have left in life to mentor someone?

_____

_____

_____

_____

_____

_____

i. http://www.managementstudyguide.com/what-is-decision-making.htm, March 11, 2013.

ii. Peterson, C., Maier, S. F., & Seligman, M. S. (1993). *Learned helplessness: A theory for the age of personal control.* Oxford: Oxford University Press.

iii. Ibid.

iv. http://www.brainyquote.com/quotes/quotes/a/antoinedes101532.html #J3Y3456r5Bs26hXM.99 October 9, 2013

v. http://www.nobelprize.org/nobel_prizes/peace/laureates/1993/mandel a-bio.html

vi. Sengel, Richard. Time magazine article titled "Mandela: His 8 Lessons of Leadership. July, 9, 2008.http://www.time.com/time/magazine/article/0,9171,1821659,00 .html Retrieved, June 21, 2013.

vii. http://thinkexist.com/quotation/those-who-do-not-move-do-not-notice-their-chains/391021.html

viii. http://www.goodreads.com/quotes/339016-a-man-devoid-of-hope-and-conscious-of-being-so Retrieved, June 21, 2013

ix. Honoring the Self: Self-Esteem and Personal Transformation. Nathaniel Branden, p. 52

x. http://thinkexist.com/quotation/courage_is_not_the_absence_of_fear-but_rather_the/220774.html. July 26, 2013

xi. http://www.statisticbrain.com/fear-of-public-speaking-statistics/, retrieved October 31, 2013

xii. After Earth, directed by M. Night Shyamalan (2013; Columbia Pictures).

xiii. http://www.goodreads.com/quotes/192269-a-coward-dies-a-thousand-times-before-his-death-but#

xiv. Steve Chandler. 100 Ways to Motivate Yourself, U.S.A. Book-mart Press, 2004, p. 62.

xv. Nathaniel Branden. The Six Pillars of Self-esteem, Random House LLC, 1995, p. 74.

xvi. http://www.brainyquote.com/quotes/quotes/r/ralphwaldo108797.ht ml

xvii. http://blog.gaiam.com/quotes/authors/guillaume-apollinaire

xviii. https://www.morehouse.edu/about/chapel/mays_wisdom.html

xix. http://www.brandeis.edu/legacyfund/bio.html

xx. http://www.goodreads.com/quotes/978-whether-you-think-you-can-or-you-think-you-can-t--you-re#

xxi. http://www.goodreads.com/quotes/287903-we-are-addicted-to-our-thoughts-we-cannot-change-anything

xxii. http://www.goodreads.com/quotes/755094-he-who-cannot-change-the-very-fabric-of-his-thought

xxiii. Hancock, David. The Secret of Master Marketing. Morgan James Publishing, 2003, p. 19.

xxiv. http://www.huffingtonpost.com/2013/01/04/cost-of-super-bowl-ad-2013_n_2410036.html

xxv. http://www.forbes.com/sites/alexkonrad/2013/02/02/even-with-record-prices-10-million-spot/

xxvi. Gladwell, Malcolm. Outliers

xxvii. http://www.goodreads.com/quotes/tag/acceptance

xxviii. http://www.goodreads.com/quotes/tag/persistence

xxix. http://www.goodreads.com/quotes/tag/patience

xxx. http://www.leadershipnow.com/integrityquotes.html

xxxi. http://www.goodreads.com/quotes/tag/integrity

xxxii. http://www.goodreads.com/quotes/tag/honor

xxxiii. http://www.biblegateway.com/passage/?search=genesis%2041&version=NIV

xxxiv. http://www.goodreads.com/quotes/11741-the-weak-can-never-forgive-forgiveness-is-the-attribute-of

xxxv. http://www.biblegateway.com/passage/?search=Genesis+45&version=NIV

xxxvi. http://www.goodreads.com/quotes/77132-true-forgiveness-is-when-you-can-say-thank-you-for

xxxvii. http://en.wikipedia.org/wiki/Aristotle

xxxviii. http://www.goodreads.com/quotes/80461-excellence-is-never-an-accident-it-is-always-the-result

xxxix. http://www.hawes.com/pastlist.htm

xl. http://www.biography.com/people/jk-rowling-40998?page=1

xli. http://www.the-leaky-cauldron.org/books/awards

xlii. http://www.biography.com/people/jk-rowling-40998?page=1

xliii. http://changeminds.wordpress.com/2011/03/20/rags-to-riches-success-story-of-jk-rowling/

xliv. http://www.youtube.com/watch?v=Pxh2sgg_iyA

xlv. http://www.bruceleefoundation.com/index.cfm/page/Biography/pid/10585

xlvi. http://www.imdb.com/title/tt0070034/business?ref_=tt_dt_bus

xlvii. http://www.biblegateway.com/passage/?search=Isaiah+55&version=NIV

xlviii. Christopher Chabris and Daniel Simons. The Invisible Gorilla: How Our Intuitions Deceive Us, Random House, LLC, 2010.

xlix. http://psychology.wikia.com/wiki/Inattentional_blindness

l. Rock, Grant, & Mack. (1992) Perceptions Without Attention: Results of a new method.

li. http://www.brainyquote.com/quotes/quotes/t/thucydides126491.html

lii. http://www.goodreads.com/quotes/10280-time-is-what-we-want-most-but-what-we-use-worst

liii. Daniel T. Willngham, Why Don't Students Like School? (San Francisco, CA: Jossey-Bass, A Wiley Imprint, 2009) p. 37.

liv. http://www.biblegateway.com/passage/?search=matthew+5&version=NIV

lv. Gardner, Howard (2000). *Intelligence Reframed: Multiple Intelligences for the 21st Century*. Basic Books Inc. p. 304. ISBN 978-0-465-02611-1.

lvi. Ibid

lvii. http://howardgardner01.files.wordpress.com/2012/06/mi-at-251.pdf

lviii. Gardner, Howard (2000), *Intelligence Reframed: Multiple Intelligences for the 21st Century*, Basic Books, ISBN 978-0-465-02611-1

lix. http://www.learning-styles-online.com/style/visual-spatial/

lx. http://school.familyeducation.com/disabled-persons/role-models/37402.html

lxi. http://surfaquarium.com/MI/profiles/visual.htm

lxii. http://www.netlingo.com/top50/popular-text-terms.php

lxiii. http://www.walb.com/story/23180074/text-message-slang-pops-up-in-classrooms

lxiv. http://www.bcps.org/offices/lis/models/tips/styles.html

lxv. http://school.familyeducation.com/disabled-persons/role-models/37398.html

lxvi. http://surfaquarium.com/MI/profiles/verbal.htm

lxvii. The David Lazear Group 2003, *A different kind of smart! A different kind of learning!*, Retrieved November 13, 2008 from http://www.miqsmart.com/Multi-Intell/index.htm

lxviii. http://school.familyeducation.com/disabled-persons/role-models/37399.html

lxix. http://surfaquarium.com/MI/profiles/logical.htm

lxx. http://school.familyeducation.com/multiple-intelligences/learning-styles/bodily-kinesthetic/66381.html

lxxi. Ednovation 2001, *The genius within: theory of multiple intelligences*, Retrieved November 13, 2008, from http://ehlt.flinders.edu.au/education/DLiT/2008/multipleintel/bodily fr.html

lxxii. http://school.familyeducation.com/disabled-persons/role-models/37396.html

lxxiii. http://surfaquarium.com/MI/profiles/kinesthetic.htm

lxxiv. McGrath, H and Noble, T 1995, *Seven ways at once*, Longman, Melbourne, from http://ehlt.flinders.edu.au/education/DLiT/2008/multipleintel/music fr.html

lxxv. http://surfaquarium.com/MI/profiles/musical.htm

lxxvi. http://school.familyeducation.com/disabled-persons/role-models/37397.html

lxxvii. http://surfaquarium.com/MI/profiles/intrapersonal.htm

lxxviii. http://school.familyeducation.com/disabled-persons/role-models/37401.html?detoured=1

lxxix. http://surfaquarium.com/MI/profiles/naturalist.htm

lxxx. http://en.wikipedia.org/wiki/Socrates

lxxxi. http://en.wikipedia.org/wiki/T._D._Jakes

lxxxii.Gardner, Howard (2000), *Intelligence Reframed: Multiple Intelligences for the 21st Century*, Basic Books, ISBN 978-0-465-02611-1

lxxxiii. http://surfaquarium.com/MI/profiles/existential.htm

lxxxiv. http://www.goodreads.com/quotes/493669-investing-in-yourself-is-the-best-investment-you-will-ever

lxxxv. http://www.goodreads.com/quotes/322401-different-roads-sometimes-lead-to-the-same-castle

lxxxvi. http://www.entheos.com/quotes/by_topic/practice

lxxxvii. http://www.forbes.com/2009/11/11/brand-defining-marketing-cmo-network-allen-adamson.html Retrieved on August 28, 2013.

lxxxviii. http://www.usatoday.com/story/money/markets/2013/12/02/why-costco-is-beating-wal-mart/3691555/

lxxxix. http://www.forbes.com/sites/rickungar/2013/04/17/walmart-pays-workers-poorly-and-sinks-while-costco-pays-workers-well-and-sails-proof-that-you-get-what-you-pay-for/

xc. http://www.merriam-webster.com/dictionary/discipline

xci. Marilyn Mandala Schlitz, Cassandra Vieten and Tina Amorok. Living Deeply: The Art and Science of Transformation in Everyday Life. 2007. New Harbinger Publication, Inc., Oakland, CA, p. 92-109.

xcii. http://www.goodreads.com/quotes/507476-do-not-imagine-that-the-good-you-intend-will-balance

xciii. Michael D. Walker, "The 7 Success Secrets: Motown," posted on April 15, 2010. http://www.thesuccesssecrets.net/the-success-secrets-motown/ (accessed September 7, 2013).

xciv. http://www.goodreads.com/author/quotes/283828.Berry_Gordy

xcv. http://www.ali.com/legend_timeline.php

xcvi. http://www.ali.com/legend_stats.php

xcvii. http://www.brainyquote.com/quotes/authors/o/oliver_wendell_holmes_jr.html

xcviii. Martin, Roger. How Successful Leaders Think. Harvard Business Review, June, 2007.

xcix. Ibid.

c. http://www.forbes.com/sites/joefolkman/2013/09/19/solving-the-decisiveness-dilemma-the-4-step-process-for-making-an-excellent-choice/

ci. http://www.brainyquote.com/quotes/authors/e/elizabeth_kenny.html

cii. http://www.forbes.com/sites/margiewarrell/2013/06/18/take-a-risk-the-odds-are-better-than-you-think/

ciii. Daniel Kahneman. Thinking fast and slow. Farrar, Straus, and Giroux. New York, 2011.

civ. http://www.happypublishing.com/blog/risk-quotes/

cv. http://www.biblegateway.com/passage/?search=Romans%208:28&version=NIV

cvi. http://en.wikipedia.org/wiki/The_Road_Not_Taken

cvii. http://www.brainyquote.com/quotes/quotes/t/tseliot161678.html

cviii. Margie Warrell. Stop Playing Safe: Rethink Risk, Unlock the power of courage. Achieve Outstanding Success. John Wiley and Sons Australia, Ltd, 2013.

cix. http://colonelsanders.com/bio.asp

cx. http://www.kfc.com/about/

cxi. Photo from www.colonelsanders.com

cxii. http://famousdaily.com/history/george-burns-signs-contract-at-87.html

cxiii. http://www.imdb.com/name/nm0122675/bio?ref_=nm_dyk_tm_sm#trademark

cxiv. Ibid

cxv. http://articles.chicagotribune.com/1986-02-02/features/8601090087_1_caesars-palace-george-burns-second-wind

cxvi. Photo from www.biography.com/people/george-burns-9232145

cxvii. Photo from http://www.fdfi.org/fd.html

cxviii. http://www.goodreads.com/quotes/278236-a-thought-is-harmless-unless-we-believe-it-it-s-not

cxix. http://www.connerpartners.com/frameworks-and-processes/the-basics-of-reframing

cxx. Photo from http://www.moillusions.com/wp-content/uploads/2012/09/Two-Face-Optical-Illusion-c.jpg

cxxi. Photo from http://www.moillusions.com/wp-
content/uploads/2012/09/Two-Face-Optical-Illusion-c.jpg

cxxii. http://www.ali.com/pdfs/timeline_ali.pdf

cxxiii. http://www.biblegateway.com/passage/?search=1%20Corinthians%
209&version=NIV

cxxiv. http://www.biblegateway.com/passage/?search=Colossians%203&v
ersion=NIV

cxxv. http://www.biblegateway.com/passage/?search=Romans%2012&ver
sion=NIV

cxxvi. http://www.biography.com/people/steve-harvey-
20631517?page=1#early-life

cxxvii. Kimbro, Dennis. The Wealth Choice: Success Secrets of Black
Millionaires. Palgrave Macmillan, 2013.

cxxviii. http://www.biography.com/people/steve-harvey-
20631517?page=1#early-life

cxxix. Ibid.

cxxx. http://smharveyfoundation.org/aboutus/

cxxxi. Ibid

cxxxii. http://www.thehistorymakers.com/biography/r-donahue-peebles-
39

cxxxiii. http://www.inc.com/magazine/20050301/howididit.html

cxxxiv. Ibid

cxxxv. http://en.wikipedia.org/wiki/R._Donahue_Peebles

cxxxvi. Ibid

cxxxvii. http://en.wikipedia.org/wiki/Harry_E._Johnson

cxxxviii. http://www.cnn.com/2011/10/14/opinion/blalock-king-
monument-history/

cxxxix. Ibid

cxl. http://www.stlamerican.com/business/local_business/article_5c78960
8-ef9c-11e0-86b9-001cc4c03286.html

cxli. http://www.huffingtonpost.com/2011/09/06/martin-luther-king-jr-
memorial-harry-johnson_n_949558.html

cxlii. Ibid

cxliii. http://rollingout.com/politics/who-gave-to-the-mlk-memorial-in-d-c-and-who-did-not-the-list-surprising/

cxliv. http://espn.go.com/blog/music/post/_/id/912/talkin-about-iverson-practice-10-years-later

cxlv. Geoff Colvin. Talent is Overrated: What Really Separates World Class Performers from Everybody Else. The Penguin Group Publishing, New York. 2008, p. 66.

cxlvi. http://www.owgr.com/. Retrieved on March 15, 2014.

cxlvii. Earl Woods with Peter McDaniel. Training a Tiger. 1997. Harper Collins.

cxlviii. Ibid.

cxlix. Ibid.

cl. Attributed to Noel Tichy, Professor of Management & Organizations at the Ross School of Business at the University of Michigan.

cli. Jerry Maguire. Director Cameron Crowe. Performance names of key actors: Tom Cruise, Cuba Gooding Jr., Renee Zellweger. TriStar Pictures, 1996.

clii. http://articles.latimes.com/1998/jan/28/news/mn-13012

cliii. Delany, Sarah L., A. Elizabeth Delany, and Amy Hill Hearth. *Having Our Say: The Delany Sisters' First 100 Years*, New York: Kodansha America, 1993.

cliv. The New York Times (archives) 1993–1995.

clv. http://www.lagcc.cuny.edu/havingoursay

clvi. http://linksvayer.bio.upenn.edu/PDFS/Linksvayer%20and%20Janssen%202008%20adaptivecapacityants.pdf

clvii. http://www.biblegateway.com/passage/?search=1%20kings%204&version=KJV

clviii. http://www.howitworksdaily.com/environment/question-of-the-day-why-can-ants-lift-so-much/

clix. http://en.wikipedia.org/wiki/Ant

clx. Carrol CR, Janzen DH (1973). "Ecology of foraging by ants". *Annual Review of Ecology and Systematics* 4: 231–257. doi:10.1146/annurev.es.04.110173.001311.

clxi. http://www.startribune.com/science/121000294.html

clxii. http://www.antsalive.com/antfaqs.htm

clxiii. http://www.merriam-webster.com/dictionary/feedback

clxiv. David Nicol & Debra Macfarlane-Dick (2006) "Formative assessment and self-regulated learning: A model and seven principles of good feedback practice" *Studies in Higher Education* vol.31 no.2 pp.199–218

clxv. http://en.wikipedia.org/wiki/Giraffe

clxvi. http://www.giraffeconservation.org/giraffe_facts.php?pgid=41

clxvii. http://www.biography.com/people/george-washington-carver-9240299

clxviii. http://leandecisions.com/2012/10/how-to-create-a-decision-checklist.html

clxix. Drucker, Peter F. "Reflections of a Social Ecologist," *Society*, May/June 1992.

clxx. http://paddyupton.com/newsletter/the-remarkable-story-of-cliff-young/

clxxi. http://www.elitefeet.com/the-legend-of-cliff-young

clxxii. Ibid

clxxiii. http://www.goodreads.com/quotes/3235-it-must-be-borne-in-mind-that-the-tragedy-of

clxxiv. Gardner, Howard (2000). *Intelligence Reframed: Multiple Intelligences for the 21st Century*. Basic Books Inc. p. 304. ISBN 978-0-465-02611-1

clxxv. Rick Pitino with Pat Forde. Rebound Rules: The Art of Success 2.0. Harper Collins e-books, p. 185.

About the Author

SAMUEL L. JONES is a professional speaker, educator, author and trainer. He is the current owner of Life Changing Presentations, a consulting company that focuses on leadership development training, strategic planning, and customer service. He is the facilitator/trainer for the Mississippi Economic Council's Leadership Mississippi program and the Dean of Student Affairs at Jones County Junior College in Ellisville, Mississippi.

Dr. Jones received a degree in Advertising and a Master's degree in Public Relations, both from the University of Southern Mississippi and a Ph.D. from Mississippi State University in Educational Leadership. After his basketball career at USM, he continued his professional basketball career in Finland. He's conducted training and seminars for organizations such as the University of Southern Mississippi's Alumni Association, Navigator Credit Union, Mississippi Power, H.O.B.Y. (Hugh O'Brian Youth Leadership), Phi Theta Kappa International, Mississippi Department of Transportation (MDOT) and the Mississippi Department of Education to name a few. He's a member of the National Speakers Association and was inducted into the University of Southern Mississippi's Alumni Hall of Fame in 2013.

Dr. Jones is married to the former Sarah Clark of Richton, MS. He is also an ordained Minister, and he serves as the Superintendent for the Sunday school at Peace and Goodwill Missionary Baptist Church in Richton, MS.

Visit the author's websites at:

www.drsamueljones.com
www.lifechangingpresentations.com

CPSIA information can be obtained
at www.ICGtesting.com
Printed in the USA
LVOW12s0030130217

524076LV00001B/208/P